Understanding
The Catcher in the Rye

The Greenwood Press "Literature in Context" Series
Student Casebooks to Issues, Sources, and Historical Documents

The Adventures of Huckleberry Finn
  by Claudia Durst Johnson

Anne Frank's *The Diary of a Young Girl*
  by Hedda Rosner Kopf

The Crucible
  by Claudia Durst Johnson and
  Vernon E. Johnson

Death of a Salesman
  by Brenda Murphy and
  Susan C. W. Abbotson

The Great Gatsby
  by Dalton Gross and
  MaryJean Gross

Hamlet
  by Richard Corum

I Know Why the Caged Bird Sings
  by Joanne Megna-Wallace

Jamaica Kincaid's *Annie John*
  by Deborah Mistron

The Literature of World War II
  by James H. Meredith

Macbeth
  by Faith Nostbakken

Of Mice and Men, The Red Pony, and
The Pearl
  by Claudia Durst Johnson

Pride and Prejudice
  by Debra Teachman

A Raisin in the Sun
  by Lynn Domina

The Red Badge of Courage
  by Claudia Durst Johnson

Richard Wright's *Black Boy*
  by Robert Felgar

The Scarlet Letter
  by Claudia Durst Johnson

Shakespeare's *Julius Caesar*
  by Thomas Derrick

A Tale of Two Cities
  by George Newlin

Things Fall Apart
  by Kalu Ogbaa

To Kill a Mockingbird
  by Claudia Durst Johnson

UNDERSTANDING
The Catcher in the Rye

A STUDENT CASEBOOK TO ISSUES, SOURCES, AND HISTORICAL DOCUMENTS

Sanford and Ann Pinsker

The Greenwood Press
"Literature in Context" Series
Claudia Durst Johnson, Series Editor

GREENWOOD PRESS
Westport, Connecticut • London

Library of Congress Cataloging-in-Publication Data

Pinsker, Sanford.
  Understanding The catcher in the rye : a student casebook to
issues, sources, and historical documents / Sanford and Ann Pinsker.
      p.   cm.—(The Greenwood Press "Literature in context"
series, ISSN 1074–598X)
  Includes bibliographical references and index.
  ISBN 0–313–30200–6 (alk. paper)
    1. Salinger, J. D. (Jerome David), 1919– Catcher in the rye.
2. Caulfield, Holden (Fictitious character)   3. Runaway teenagers in
literature.   4. Teenage boys in literature.   I. Pinsker, Ann.
II. Title.   III. Series.
PS3537.A426C362   1999
813'.54—dc21   98–55339

British Library Cataloguing in Publication Data is available.

Library of Congress Catalog Card Number: 98–55339
ISBN: 0–313–30200–6
ISSN: 1074–598X

First published in 1999

Greenwood Press, 88 Post Road West, Westport, CT 06881
An imprint of Greenwood Publishing Group, Inc.
www.greenwood.com

Printed in the United States of America

The paper used in this book complies with the
Permanent Paper Standard issued by the National
Information Standards Organization (Z39.48–1984).

10 9 8 7 6 5 4 3 2 1

Copyright Acknowledgments

The authors and the publisher gratefully acknowledge permission to use the following material:

Excerpts from "Catcher Comes of Age" by Adam Moss, with quotes by John Updike, Peter DeVries, and Tom Wolfe, printed in *Esquire*, December 1981. By permission of Esquire magazine. © Hearst Communications, Inc. Also, Esquire is a trademark of Hearst Magazines Property, Inc. All Rights Reserved.

Excerpts from "Censorship and the Values of Fiction" by Wayne C. Booth in *The English Journal*, March 1964. Reprinted with permission.

Excerpts from *Censors in the Classroom: The Mind Benders* by Edward B. Jenkinson (Carbondale: Southern Illinois University Press, 1979). Reprinted with permission.

"Censorship or Choice? Catcher in the Spotlight" by Jingle Davis in the *Atlanta Constitution*, February 10, 1997. Reprinted with permission.

"Glynn Board Votes to Keep Catcher in Its Classrooms" by Jingle Davis in the *Atlanta Constitution*, February 11, 1997. Reprinted with permission.

"Catcher Pulled from Course, Not District" by Carlos Alcala in the *Sacramento Bee*, May 2, 1997. Reprinted with permission.

"Why High School Students Should Read the Classics First" by Timothy May in the *Sacramento Bee*, May 4, 1997. Reprinted by permission of the author.

Excerpts from *The Fifties: The Way We Really Were* by Douglas T. Miller and Marion Nowak (New York: Doubleday, 1977). Reprinted with permission.

Excerpts from "Women in the Sixties" by Martha C. Nussbaum, from *Reassessing the Sixties: Debating the Political and Cultural Legacy* by Stephen Macedo, editor. Copyright © 1997 by W. W. Norton & Company, Inc. Reprinted by permission of W. W. Norton & Company, Inc.

From *Preparing for Power: America's Elite Boarding Schools* by Peter W. Cookson and Caroline Hodges Persell. Copyright © 1985 by Peter W. Cookson and Caroline Hodges Persell. Reprinted by permission of Basic Books, a member of Perseus Books, L.L.C.

Excerpts from "Pencey Preppy: Cultural Codes in *The Catcher in the Rye*" by Christopher Brookeman in *New Essays on The Catcher in the Rye*, Jack Slazman, editor (New York: Cambridge University Press, 1991). Reprinted with permission.

Excerpts from Carl R. Green and William R. Sanford's *Psychology: A Way to Grow*, reprinted by permission of Amsco School Publications, Inc.

Excerpts from *Introduction to Psychology* by Ann L. Weber. Copyright © 1991 by HarperCollins Publishers, Inc. Reprinted by permission of HarperCollins Publishers, Inc.

From *Psychology & You*, 2nd edition, by Frank B. McMahon, Judith W. McMahon, and Tony Romano, editors. © 1995. Reprinted with permission of South-Western Educational Publishing, a division of International Thomson Publishing. Fax 800 730-2215.

"A Much Riskier Passage" by David Gelman. From *Newsweek*, summer/fall 1990. © 1990, Newsweek, Inc. All rights reserved. Reprinted by permission.

Every reasonable effort has been made to trace the owners of copyright materials in this book, but in some instances this has proven impossible. The authors and publisher will be glad to receive information leading to more complete acknowledgments in subsequent printings of the book and in the meantime extend their apologies for any omissions.

For our children,
who sometimes wondered
if the marriage would end before the book was finished

Contents

x   Contents

Acknowledgments

The authors would like to thank the administrations of J. P. Mc-Caskey High School and Franklin and Marshall College for their encouragement. Tom Karel of Franklin and Marshall College's Shadek-Fackenthal Library was helpful beyond our capacity to thank him, as was his daughter, Anastasia, who served as our research assistant. We also wish to acknowledge the helpful suggestions and generous assistance of the following people: Pam Bradley, Mark Pinsker, Mel Ruth, David Schuyler, and David Zubatsky. Finally, at Greenwood Publishing Group, Elizabeth Meagher, Claudia Durst Johnson, and Barbara Rader did their best to make sure that we crossed our i's and dotted our t's. Any mistakes that slipped through these nets are our own.

Introduction

The Catcher in the Rye is unquestionably one of the most widely read, most influential, and most controversial novels in contemporary American literature. No other literary work seems better able to capture the pressures and tensions of prep school life, the confusions of late adolescence, the quest for a vaguely defined religious purity, or the contradictions that result when its protagonist too neatly divides the world into phonies, on one hand, and the pure in spirit, on the other. In this sense, Salinger's portrait of Holden Caulfield remains as compelling and as fresh today as it was when it first appeared in 1951. Successive generations of high school students have followed his adventures in Manhattan with fascination and often with large measures of empathy. For many, Holden is *them*, however much the essential details may differ. Why so? Because what Salinger has done is neither more nor less than to have invented a character, somebody we know (or think we know) down to the soles of his shoes: how his "voice" sounds; what he wears; what his "take" on the world is; and, perhaps most of all, what he thinks. In a word, this character breathes in the way that (usually) only live persons do.

At the same time, however, Holden Caulfield is a reflection of the sociocultural conditions of his age, one defined by post–World War II affluence and angst, by large movements toward conformity and small gestures of rebellion. As such, Holden shapes and is shaped by cultural attitudes he both sharply criticizes and unknowingly embraces. Ironically, he is often seen as a child of the 1950s, even though the decade had scarcely begun when he set about narrating his tale of woe at Pencey Prep and the "madman weekend" he spent in Manhattan after being expelled. He is at once "us" as the 1950s defined us and much larger, much more universal than any specific time or place.

The identification of character and decade, however, is not without merit—for Holden, perhaps more than any other literary figure of the period, has become part of our collective unconscious. He stands as a foreshadowing of a time when bland conformity and materialistic values would collide with versions of spiritual resistance and radical individualism. He stands as well for the subversive spirit that has been part of serious American literature from its beginnings. One thinks of Nathaniel Hawthorne's double-edged vision of American Puritanism in *The Scarlet Letter*, of Herman Melville's "Bartleby the Scrivener," a story that pits an alienated man against the world of business, or Walt Whitman's radically egalitarian poetic vision. Most of all, however, one thinks of Mark Twain's *Adventures of Huckleberry Finn*, a novel in which a fourteen-year-old boy accurately and satirically describes the social evil and personal corruption of the antebellum South.

As with Huck, Holden Caulfield makes sharp, often penetrating commentary about his society and its entrenched hypocrisies. Not surprisingly, many adults worried about Holden's strong appeal to young readers. For some, the issue was his language, peppered throughout by mild obscenities and, in some places, by words that have no place in high school courses or libraries; for others, Holden was a subversive character who raised disturbing questions about adult authority, school discipline and spirit, and, perhaps most of all, the importance of learning how to accommodate, to play Life's "game" with effectiveness and purpose. In short, Holden's radical individuality often seemed to call the entire social fabric into doubt.

Meanwhile, the popularity of *The Catcher in the Rye* continues. For the young, it is less a novel than a rite of passage, something that one generation after another of high school students continue to read despite the competition of MTV and video games. In Woody Allen's *Mighty Aphrodite*, a Manhattan couple speculates about possible names for their newly adopted infant son. One of them, perhaps not surprisingly, is Holden. Adults of a certain age caught the allusion, but so, too, did many youngsters in the audience. This is because the issues that the novel raises are universal enough, *timeless* enough, to transcend the boundaries of age, place, or condition.

During this study of *The Catcher in the Rye*, the reader will encounter a great many questions. They are designed less to generate specific answers than to prod deeper thinking about how to read this novel (and, indeed, many other serious novels), by adding supplementary material to a close encounter with the book itself. To better understand how this strategy works, let us begin by contemplating a fundamental issue in the ongoing debate about how novels such as *The Catcher in the Rye* should be studied:

- Should *The Catcher in the Rye* be studied as a self-contained unit? By that we mean, does Salinger provide, *within the work*, all the information a reader needs to "study" his novel? How important are the various allusions that Holden makes to Hollywood films or to specific authors and books? Is it possible to read Salinger's novel without knowing the full context of these allusions, or would the novel be enriched by widening the scope of one's study?

- More specifically, should readers of *The Catcher in the Rye* confine themselves to a searching analysis of the novel only? What would be the benefits of such an approach? What might some of the liabilities include?

- Would it enhance a student's understanding of the work to go beyond the author and story to learn more about its affinities to *Adventures of Huckleberry Finn*, the literary/cultural allusions sprinkled throughout the novel, or the controversies the book has created? Maybe using the example of an obviously social work like *The Catcher in the Rye* loads the argument in favor of including background information, but it is hard to think of novels that are *not* social. Still, it may be true that some works of literature are more readily studied as self-contained entities than others.

- Are there certain short stories, novels, plays, poems, or film scripts that could or even *should* be considered without reference to issues and information outside the work itself? What would some examples be, and is there perhaps a difference between an impressionist reaction to a work of literature and a richer, more considered reading?

- Are one's impressions (e.g., "I like Holden"; "I just hate that guy") sufficient? The fancy name for this phenomenon is "reader-response theory," but one need not know about aesthetic squabbles to realize that a work of art comes to life only when somebody "looks" at a painting or hears a piece of music. The same thing is true for a novel, which, the argument would have it, comes to life only when an individual reader turns the pages. In the triangle of novel, cultural setting, and reader, such critics emphasize the reader.

As you read and study, an ever-increasing amount of literature, your inclination about these questions will probably change. Experience is, in this sense, a powerful teacher; and what may seem a difficult business—namely, finding the "best" way to approach a work of literature—will become fairly simple.

In this study, we begin with an overview of *The Catcher in the Rye*, that focuses on the novel's themes, characters, and literary techniques. Subsequently, however, we broaden these traditional literary approaches to include issues and items of historical background that are external to the novel itself. We do this as a way of deepening a reader's understanding of the novel itself.

Our approach is interdisciplinary. That is, the materials we provide to accompany our study of the novel come from a variety of disciplines: history, popular culture, sociology, and legal studies—not just literary criticism, the discipline that merely opens the inquiry at hand. The assumption on which this volume rests is that in the social and historical background of the novel, one can find useful issues for analysis of a literary text.

Besides all this, we think that such a broad approach to the literary text enlarges a reader's understanding of both past and present—the history out of which the fiction emerges as well as the enduring issues that are part of the fabric of the fiction.

The broad questions raised about the novel by the documents in this collection are as follows:

- How can the form and themes of *The Catcher in the Rye* be viewed independently of all other considerations?
- How does information about the conformity of post–World War

II America (the time of the novel's setting) shed light on Holden's rebellious attitudes?

- Does a growing sense of materialism, as documented in the source materials, always accompany a decline in spiritual-religious sensitivity?

- How does the fact that Holden is a Manhattanite affect his characteristic speech and cultural attitudes? How are these identifying traits transcended (if, indeed, they are) by the tone and texture of the novel?

- In what ways do the peculiar tensions of modern life (e.g., the Cold War, the atomic bomb) contribute to Holden's dilemma?

- Is Holden an extended portrait of what some have regarded as a spoiled rich kid, or are these details less important than his fascination with what might be called "the death question"?

- How does information about censorship in schools and libraries in general and censorship of this novel in particular throw light on the theme, tone, and language of the novel?

A variety of different records are excerpted here as source material for our study of *The Catcher in the Rye*:

- Supreme Court cases on censorship
- newspaper articles
- psychological profiles of adolescent development
- interviews
- historical and sociological studies
- selected movie reviews
- magazine articles
- biographical material

In each instance, the source materials have been selected to work with the fictional creation, the novel, to bring past and present issues into sharper focus. In addition to the documents, each selection of the text contains (1) an introductory discussion, (2) study questions, (3) topics for writing or oral exploration, and (4) a list of suggested readings.

1

Literary Analysis

Holden Caulfield's now famous opening line in which he reluctantly addresses the sort of things he imagines his readers will be interested in—where he was born and how he spent his childhood, what his parents do for a living, and lots of other personal background material—establishes the general tone in which Holden will tell the story of his adventures in Manhattan during a fateful weekend. In addition, Holden's vernacular opening lines announce *The Catcher in the Rye*'s kinship with other narrative fictions that also employ a retrospective first-person narrator (Herman Melville's *Moby-Dick*, Mark Twain's *Adventures of Huckleberry Finn*, F. Scott Fitzgerald's *The Great Gatsby*, and Ralph Ellison's *The Invisible Man*).

Consider, for example, the difference between Holden's narrative stance and the one it most self-consciously echoes: the opening salvo of *Adventures of Huckleberry Finn*: "You don't know about me, without you have read a book by the name of 'The Adventures of Tom Sawyer,' but that ain't no matter." Huck Finn is a battered child, while it could be argued that Holden has been spoiled rotten; Huck has no illusions about his ignorance, while Holden peppers his chatter with Scholastic Aptitude Test (SAT) words like "ostracized"; and most important of all, while Huck's "adventures" alter him significantly (he is not the same patsy in the novel's last paragraphs that he was throughout his sojourn south), many critics point out that Holden remains the same self-indulgent romantic he always was.

What Huck and Holden share, however—aside from their respective initiations into the variety and the viciousness of adult corruption—is the mutual condition of being protagonists in death-haunted novels. Hardly a page of either book is spared the taint of mortality, whether it expresses itself in the chivalric, ultimately deadly rhetoric of the Grangerfords or in Holden's exam essay on Egyptian mummies; in the grisly specter of Huck's dead friend, Buck, or in Holden's haunting memories of his older brother Allie; in Huck's conviction that "an owl, away off, who-whooing [is] about somebody that was going to die"; or in Holden's quick leap from a magazine article about the warning signs of cancer to the certainty of the grave. Holden has a rich imagination when it comes to the gloomy. He fattens on troubles—some real enough, others largely cooked up for the occasion.

Moreover, Holden's speech is filled with slang that can be read simultaneously on two levels. When, for example, he points out that this or that "killed him" (usually with reference to the surprising politeness or just plain whimsy in children), the phrase cannot help but call our attention to his brooding obsession about his brother Allie's death and, indeed, about death in general. When Phoebe, Holden's younger sister, points out that "Daddy'll kill you!" (because Holden has flunked out of yet another prep school), the point is less that there is an oedipal struggle going on in the Caulfields' expensive Manhattan apartment than that this is the hyperbolic way teenagers actually speak. (As the novel makes abundantly clear, Holden harbors no competitive, much less murderous, thoughts about his father; and the same thing is true about Mr. Caulfield to Holden. They are, in short, hardly cast as Mrs. Caulfield's jealous lovers, nor do they bear the slightest resemblance either to characters in the Sophocles's *Oedipus Rex* or to the case histories of Freud.) Salinger chooses such words with care—again, not because he has an oedipal card up his sleeve, but rather because Holden's capacity to disappoint his parents' expectations is one strand in a much larger pattern of death imagery. That Holden has managed to flunk out of yet another prep school is the stuff that parental disapproval is made of; indeed, Phoebe imagines that it will come to a shouting match. Not surprisingly,

Holden is worried about the same thing, although his more immediate concern is the world that is, in poet William Wordsworth's phrase, "too much with him."

Huck and Holden also share in the loneliness that is an inextricable by-product of their respective broodings, for isolation is built into the territory of their retrospective narratives. Granted, Huck bonds with the adult slave Jim in those resplendent, short-lived scenes in which man, boy, and raft merge with the river. Holden is less fortunate, for in a world where phonies vastly outnumber the pure of heart, there are only thin pockets of stasis: unspoiled, white snow, the Museum of Natural History, Phoebe in her blue coat going round and round on the Central Park carousel: Everything else is a veritable flood tide pushing Holden toward change, toward adulthood, toward responsibility, toward abject phoniness, and, of course, toward death.

By contrast, Holden's story is filled with what his Oral Expression class is taught to call "digressions." Rather than proceeding in a straight, chronological line, he wanders—first announcing that he will relate the story of his exhausting, even mad adventures during a weekend sojourn in Manhattan last Christmas and then pausing to include more information about his older brother D. B. than the situation requires.

Holden's casual leaps and associative jumps come with the territory of adolescence and help to establish his credibility as the novel's seventeen-year-old narrator. But the extended asides also give Salinger an opportunity to move from Holden's penchant for hyperbole (for example, he claims that his brother's Jaguar is capable of speeds in the 200-mile per hour range) to his various—and uncompromising—sociomoral stands. It's bad enough that D. B. drives a pretentious car but much worse that he can afford it (and much else) now that he is making "heaps" of money as a screenwriter in Hollywood. This was not always the case. When D. B. was relatively poor (and certainly unspoiled), he had written what Holden regards as a terrific book of short stories called *The Secret Goldfish*. The title story, about a child who wouldn't allow anybody to look at his goldfish because he had bought it with his own money and it was *his*, has the look and feel of the work that Salinger would later publish as *Nine Stories*.

The Catcher in the Rye gives us very little information about "The Secret Goldfish"—neither an extended plot summary nor a few snippets of its style—but we know that it belongs to Salinger's imaginative world nonetheless. According to Holden, when D. B. wrote that story, he was a *writer*; now, entangled in Hollywood, he has become, in Holden's telling word, a "prostitute" and, perhaps even worse, somebody who can be counted among the phonies.

In short, the movies have ruined D. B., just as Holden remains convinced that the movies ruin everybody else. Why so? Because, as far as he is concerned, movie actors are *acting*. They do not believe the lines they so carefully rehearse because, in the theater and motion pictures, illusion is more important than reality. All of which makes his enthusiastic reading of "The Secret Goldfish" and his disapproval of D. B.'s work in Hollywood somewhat problematic. One suspects that Holden would be quick to censure the adult who refused to let anybody look at, say, his hard-earned BMW (children are quite another matter) or that he protests a bit too much about his professed hatred of the movies. For one who knocks the flicks, he certainly spends a good deal of his time taking them in. The point is that Salinger's protagonist prefers the innocence and "secrets" of childhood to the world of getting-and-spending where writers give up private goldfish for Hollywood cash. Thus, D. B. gets written off in a single, judgmental word: *prostitute*. But the digression serves yet another strategic purpose, namely to postpone telling readers that his story *properly* begins on the fateful day when failing marks require that he leave Pencey Prep. Granted, Holden has been booted out of schools twice before, but despite Holden's best efforts at evasion—he claims that he simply forgot about getting sacked from Pencey Prep—or the dry, matter-of-fact way he recounts how his academic fate unrolled, the banishment hurts—all the more so because he realizes that the warning voices at midterm were right: he had not applied himself. In this sense, Holden is hardly a prototype of the brash, chest-thumping Bart Simpson. Salinger's protagonist may well be numbered among the prep school world's more conspicuous "underachievers" (a term that did not exist in Holden's day), but he is certainly not proud of the fact. Indeed, his elaborate efforts at justification fall just short of apology, and his vivid memories from his days at Elkton Hills and Whooten make it clear—long before the novel's last paragraph—that he "misses" the people he has been forced to leave.

Still, as Holden himself readily admits, he just couldn't get around the application business. The rub is that *applying* yourself is precisely how you later turn into a phony. At Pencey, students are expected to play the game, whether it be a football contest pitting Pencey against Saxon Hall (where winning, Holden argues, is a matter of life and death) or what Dr. Thurmer, Pencey's headmaster, calls the larger "game of Life." About these and many other platitudes that adults try to fob off to teenagers, Holden has his cynical doubts. If you happen to find yourself on the side where all the "hotshots" are, then it's a game; but, he goes on to point out, what about the people on the other side? Holden is talking about himself, as well as about all those too innocent, too pure of heart to become hotshots. For them, life ends up being no game at all. That Holden's sees this truth is part of what makes him an appealing character and also what causes him extraordinary psychic pain.

However much Holden's sentiments seem an echo of Frederic Henry's bitter comments about the absurdities of war in Hemingway's *A Farewell to Arms* (1929) ("If they catch you off base, they kill you"), there are important differences. At one point, Holden mentions *A Farewell to Arms* specifically, wondering why D. B. could hate war and still admire a phony like Lieutenant Henry. Granted, Holden applies a rather curious litmus test to literature (he "approves" of characters who agree with him and tends to dismiss those who don't—and this is especially true if they strike him as contradictory and/or hypocritical). Holden prefers characters who "knock him out" with small touches and childlike gestures and authors who create the impression that they are friendly, altogether nice folks you could call up on the telephone. One such author would not be Salinger himself, famous for his reclusiveness and absolute unavailability for interviews, book signings, public lectures, and, most of all, telephone calls from fans like Holden.

But life-as-game is not the only place where Salinger dwells on sports. In point of fact, however, *The Catcher in the Rye* is filled with references to sports in general and to some games in particular. There are, for example, references to ice skating (the ill-fated date that takes Holden and Sally Hayes to the rink at Rockefeller Center), to roller skating (Holden makes much of the skate key he uses when he tightens a young girl's skates), to golf (Holden was presumably so good at the game he was once asked to be in a movie short; being Holden, he refused—partly because it would be hypocritical, given his severe criticisms of motion pictures, and partly because Holden has an instinctive aversion to competition per se), and to the ritualistic football matches as well as the equally ritualistic games of checkers he remembers playing with Jane Gallagher. But when Holden tallies the respective scores, it's always the same: hotshots: everything, non-hotshots: nothing. *Games*, in short, are always rigged games, especially if you happen to be on the perpetually losing side.

If competitive sport is simply warfare under another name, it is worth pointing out that Holden finds himself surrounded by the imagery of battle: the "crazy cannon" he leans against as he watches the respective football teams clash against each other on Pencey's darkling plain, the fencing foils he "accidentally" leaves on the subway, and, perhaps most of all, his confrontation with Mr. Spencer, the history teacher who lives on Anthony Wayne Avenue. Indeed, reminders of the American Revolution are scattered across Pencey's well-manicured turf, and not merely to provide an appropriate local coloring, for Holden is engaged in nothing less than a contemporary revolution against authority figures that he may not completely understand, but with no shortage of enemies. Even the war hero's nickname—"Mad" Anthony Wayne—is carefully chosen as yet another indicator, or *nuance*, of all that is "crazy" in a novel that pits those who are sane, but phony, against those who are pure, but headed for nervous breakdowns.

The well-meaning Mr. Spencer—distressed because he has had to flunk Holden in history—stands for what passes, in Pencey and elsewhere, as sanity, for filling in the blanks correctly and for writing dutiful (read: conventional) themes, despite his address on Anthony Wayne Avenue. He had written Holden a note asking to see him before he left Pencey; and because Holden is a great believer in proper farewells, he feels a double obligation to show up. But Spencer is destined to become yet another bead in Holden's long string of disappointments. For one thing, the Spencers are, by Holden's glib economic reckoning, *poor*: without a butler, *they* must answer knocks at the door; without a maid, Mrs. Spencer *herself* must serve whatever refreshments their meager funds can afford.

Moreover, Mr. Spencer is, like the history he teaches, *old*; and that fact alone is enough to occasion at least a portion of Holden's contempt. He can't quite figure out what Mr. Spencer is living for, because the vagaries of age have made him so stoop-shouldered that whenever he drops a piece of chalk on the floor, a student has to pick it up for him. Such pathetic creatures have no place in Holden's world; they simply take up room better left for the innocent and the young.

To make matters even worse, Mr. Spencer is sick, surrounded by medicines and confined to a room that reeks of Vicks Nose Drops. All this makes Holden uncomfortable and fuels many of his snide observations about the elderly. The scene unrolls, with the bathrobed, bumpy-chested Mr. Spencer on one side and Holden— forced to sit on his teacher's bed—on the other. The result is a classic instance of crossed purposes and missed communication, of Innocence pitted against Authority.

Mr. Spencer is obviously disturbed by having to fail a Pencey student, especially if his grade contributed to the boy's being expelled; but he is also interested in exonerating himself, in getting the student in question to admit that he as a teacher had no other choice, that what he did was *right*. The trouble is that the "student in question" is Holden Caulfield. Rather than argue with Mr. Spencer about his mark, Holden freely admits that he knew (in Spencer's words) "absolutely nothing" about history and that, at best, he had merely skimmed the textbook instead of trying to master it. All the while, however, he continues to makes mental notes that either confirm his previous judgment of Spencer as a man of annoying habits (he is a compulsive "nodder") or add new, undercutting information—for example, he is also a nose-picker.

If one definition of the artist is a person who cannot *not* see, who is at once blessed and cursed by an uncanny ability to observe particulars, then Holden is surely something of an artist. At the same time, however, he is also the prototypical rebel, for beneath his prep school facade and conciliatory prep school manners lies the heart of an uncompromising purist. In short, Holden is a young man as divided as he is confused. He can readily admit, for example, that he sometimes acts like a thirteen-year-old but that he has the graying hair of somebody much older. Moreover, he makes much of the fact that he stands six foot two and a half. Holden's self-descriptions are a study in ambivalence and contradiction. He worries about the changes, the mutability, that the future represents and desperately wants to "believe" in redemption, but not in the ways that Mr. Spencer would understand. What Holden sees, and worries about, are the phonies that make life limited and sad.

Granted, Holden tends to gild the lilies he offers up as proof that phonies run the whole show. Take Ossenburger, for example, a wealthy Pencey alumnus who gave a ceremonial address to the school. So far as Holden is concerned, Ossenburger never had a chance—not after he arrived at the school driving a Cadillac. On the other hand, however, even sympathetic readers soon learn to take Holden's geometry of exaggeration into account as the character remembers Ossenburger's speech lasting "about ten hours" and starting off with "about fifty corny jokes." Like his recurrent "and all," we learn to associate such verbal tics with Holden's impatience, imprecision, and, most of all, his version of the vernacular. Such stuff fills in the uneasy gaps between one Holden impression and the next.

Exaggerations of this type travel under the wide umbrella called slang. Outright *lies* are another matter, and many readers who can sympathize easily with Holden's penchant for excess have little patience with his wholesale misrepresentation of the facts. How is one to "believe" such a character, especially since everything is filtered through his unreliable sensibility? What is one to make of a first-person narrator who freely admits that he is a terrific liar and that if somebody asks him where he's going, he's more likely to lie and say he's off to the opera than to say he's headed toward the corner store to buy a magazine? Salinger's novel gives us no indication if Holden is, in fact, an opera buff (one suspects that he isn't; if theater and film are phony, wouldn't opera's sensationalist plotlines and oversized gestures be even worse?); rather, Holden enjoys putting would-be antagonists off the scent. The result is playful lies that differ markedly from the ones that adults tell.

Holden's "stretchers"—as Huck Finn, another pretty terrific liar, might describe them—are not cut from the same phony cloth as the lies that adults tell each other and, more important, that they tell to themselves. For Holden, much of life is frittered away in the trivial, in the boring; and in that sense, what could be a more *boring* question than "Where are you going?"—especially if the truthful answer is something as mundane as buying a magazine? By contrast, a Holden Caulfield who just "happens" to be going to the opera is, by definition, a more interesting character than his questioner.

Often, Holden's whoppers are designed either to spare somebody else's feelings (he told Mr. Spencer that he had to get some of his sports equipment from the gym, rather than telling him the bald truth: he had just about enough of the teacher's browbeating), or to keep the grimmer aspects of life—fears of death, of innocence's corruption, of profound loneliness—at arm's length. Holden's penchant for exaggeration operates on many of the same frequencies. Adolescents tend to think that *all* classes, and certainly all *lectures*, run longer than they actually do; and in this sense the details encrusted in Holden's paragraph about Ossenburger's speech strike the proper, realistic chords. But one also suspects that Holden is the only Pencey student barking out an obligatory "locomotive" football cheer who sees the moment for the sham it surely is. For the others, such displays of school spirit come with the territory of football games—as, for that matter, does a well-heeled donor like Ossenburger. Neither is worth a second thought, much less Holden's obsessively self-righteous tirade.

Holden is on an ill-defined quest, and his fellow classmates are not. In this sense, Holden's red hunting cap is both concrete evidence of how he doesn't fit into the Pencey mold and a symbol of the backwards hunt he will pursue in the wilds of Manhattan. Ironically enough, it is also one of the few details that have dated rather badly since the novel was first published, for in the early 1950s no self-respecting preppy would have sported an "army & navy store" hunting cap, and he certainly wouldn't have worn it as Holden did, with the peak turned backward. Thus, Holden's cap is a measure of his studied nonconformity, the way he costumes himself to make a point. His cap, he proudly declares, is of the people-killing kind—even if the claim is longer on rhetoric than reality.

Now caps with their rims reversed are commonplace, precisely the way with-it preppies march themselves to class. What hasn't changed, however, is the distinctiveness of Holden's explanation that his is a "people-shooting hat"—not, to be sure, in the literal sense that he means to take up weapons and have it out with the phonies but rather that his backwards quest will be made on behalf of innocence and that he is prepared to blow away the opposition psychologically. Does Holden realize all this at the moment he pulls Robert Ackley's leg with his off-the-wall explanation? Of course not, but, like much of what Holden says, truth speaks through the thin veil of put-downs and high jinks.

Ackley belongs to that class of people who are quickly tabbed as "losers" by others and then turn into pariahs. For such people— one thinks of Selma Thurmer, the headmaster's daughter, with her big nose and bitten-down fingernails—Holden can tick off flaws with an uncanny accuracy and still find room for compassion. Granted, poor Selma is an easier case (she could make good conversation and knew that her father was a phony), but even Ackley, despite his laundry list of faults, is not beyond the pale. Why so? Because encrusted in Holden's description of all that is unsavory, unpleasant, and just plain annoying about Ackley is also Holden's recognition of a fellow loner, somebody whose nastiness is simultaneously overcompensation and defense.

Ackley (whose very name suggests a play on "acne") is a public nuisance and a public slob. By contrast, Ward Stradlater, Holden's roommate, is the sort of boy that schools like Pencey are made for: good looking, athletic, well-rounded, and, above all else, absolutely "normal." That Holden sees through Stradlater's facade is testimony to his highly developed instinct for sniffing out undercutting details. He points out, for example, that Stradlater is a chronically bad whistler and, moreover, that he has the annoying habit of picking songs that are hard to whistle even if one were a better whistler than Stradlater. His inept versions of "Song of India" or "Slaughter on Tenth Avenue" drive Holden nuts. Even more damaging, however, is Holden's conviction that Stradlater is a "secret slob": somebody who dolls himself up in the bathroom but who leaves a razor full of lather and hairs. Those who see Stradlater in public assume that he's a good-looking, well-groomed guy; but they are wrong. If "The Secret Goldfish" is an example of the good secret, Stradlater's secret slobbiness is a telling instance of the bad one. Stradlater, in a word, is a *fake*, however much Holden secretly (that word again) admires him.

Some young readers ask themselves, "What if Holden Caulfield were *my* roommate?" and then imagine the following answer: "He'd *like* me, of course—because I'm *not* like Stradlater, *not* like Ackley. I'm caring and sensitive and, above all else, *authentic*." What this speculation leaves out is an understanding of how Holden's undercutting vision actually works. With the exception of his dead brother Allie and his sister Phoebe, the chances of *not* being written off as a phony are very slim indeed. As the truism would have it, great art is in the "details," and whatever else Holden might be, he is a young man who is relentlessly uncompromising about the small tics and generally unnoticed details that are the stuff of which phoniness is made. Holden, were he, in fact, able to be somebody other than Stradlater's roommate, would be not only a disappointment but also a disaster. That he would find indicators of phoniness—and even the smallest whiff is enough to set off his highly sensitive "phony detector"—in yet another Pencey student, in me, in *you* is clear from Salinger's text; it is also one of life's more certain truths that people find what they are looking for, be they critics hunting symbols or someone like Holden out to uncover phonies. To understand fully why this is so is to begin a serious reading of the novel Salinger intended and wrote.

Stradlater can only come off badly when compared to the memories of Allie, but it is not merely that he is a lousy whistler, a "secret slob" with a dirty razor, or even the sort of person who borrows your sports coat and then stretches out the shoulders; rather, it is that Stradlater's good looks and egomaniacal self-confidence have a sexual dimension, and on Holden's last night at Pencey, Stradlater has a date with Jane Gallagher, a girl Holden respects and is more than half in love with. Holden *cares* for her in ways that the self-centered, sexually aggressive Stradlater cannot. After all, Holden used to play checkers with her, and what he remembers most about these idyllic moments from his past is that Jane refused to move any of her kings. Rather, she would line them up in the back row and simply admire them.

Not surprisingly, Stradlater can't understand either why Holden should be so curious about whether or not Jane asked about him, or why the way she played checkers is so important. Who gives a hoot about checkers? But for Holden, Jane Gallagher's kings in the back row are rather like the purity of snow in winter: white, unsullied, and, in Holden's word, "nice." In the arithmetic of Salinger's symbolism, they suggest an aversion to risk, a need to be protected—for if Jane moves her king onto the playing field of a checkerboard, it might, after all, be *jumped*. One could argue that the whole *point* of getting a king is to use it—to jump other players and thus win the game. But Jane—as with Holden and presumably with Salinger himself—has problems with the common sense of competition; she doesn't have a bloodthirsty bone in her checker-moving hand. Besides, there is something nice, something static about such an arrangement that motion and change can only spoil. For all his bluster about wanting to be—and be treated as—an adult, what Holden desires even more deeply is for childhood memories (such as those of playing checkers with Jane) to remain forever.

Readers need not be doctrinaire Freudians to see the sexual dimension of the Caulfield/Gallagher checker games, however muted by the essential innocence of that time, that place. The present, however, is a "checker game" of an entirely different color. Holden knows Stradlater's reputation as a make-out artist, and he cannot help but imagine Jane falling hopelessly into his sex-crazed arms. What Holden fears is that Jane will move her kings out of the back row and that Stradlater will "jump" her, that she will no longer be the sad, virginal girl he once loved. Indeed, even Holden's best, most elaborate efforts to assure himself that Stradlater won't get to first base with Jane and that she is cut from very different cloth from the other girls seduced easily (much *too* easily) by good looks and smooth patter have a way of falling flat and keeping his deepest fear about the new (read: ruined) Jane Gallagher alive.

So, Holden begins the first in a series of ill-fated, increasingly desperate, and sadly comic efforts to be the savior of innocents. When Stradlater returns from his date, Holden launches into a self-styled inquisition that begins by asking him if Jane still kept her kings in the back row and then quickly cuts to the chase, namely, did Stradlater have his way with Jane in the backseat of Ed Banky's car? That Holden should move from "fightin' words" to actually *fighting* is, under the circumstances, hardly surprising; that the gesture should prove so pathetic (he aims a punch at Stradlater's throat but misses) is equally predictable. Holden is clearly no match for the larger, more physical Stradlater who puts up with Holden's initial assault (easily pinning him to the bathroom floor), but who loses his temper and proceeds to belt Holden when called a "moron." Holden hits the floor again—this time with his nose bloodied but his righteous indignation largely intact.

Holden is cut from antiheroic cloth; and as the gap between intention and result widens, as he takes a cold, hard look at himself in the bathroom mirror, he begins to realize, first, how ridiculous he now looks in his red hunting cap and, then, to admit how lonely he, in fact, is. Later Holden will talk about Pencey almost exclusively in terms of how phony such prep schools in general are, but it is his failure to stand up for Jane Gallagher, to protect both her kings and her virginity from the likes of Stradlater, that prompts his abrupt, late-night departure.

However, before his dramatic exit—one as ironically undercut as his "fight" with Stradlater—Holden spends a few revealing moments with Ackley. After all, if Ackley practically lives in *his* room, it seems only right that he should make himself comfortable in Ackley's. Besides, how can Holden return to a room he shares with a moron like Stradlater? Not surprisingly, Ackley rather resents Holden's intrusion, and things go from bad to worse when Holden brings up the delicate matter of religion, wondering what it takes to join a monastery and whether or not he would have to be a Catholic to do so. For Ackley, Holden's impertinent questions cross the line, but they speak to a religious quest that will continue, in one form or another, throughout the novel. What these assorted quests generally come to are (1) a desire for a safe, protected place outside the corrupt world, and (2) an intimation that there is a God who will watch over Holden, his sister, and his dead brother.

The vision of a cloistered life without phonies and, more important, beyond the reach of worldly corruption is not unlike Holden's dream of a world where a Jane Gallagher keeps her kings in the back row forever. Both demand that Holden renounce the flesh, and he is at least curious about the possibility. However, Ackley, being Ackley, misinterprets Holden's motive, making it clear that he doesn't particularly care what Holden says about him but that cracks about his religion are off-limits.

Still, Holden is more than half serious about halting the clock that pushes him inexorably toward adulthood. It is yet another instance of his much-threatened innocence, of Holden's desperately trying to fend off the mutability that he associates with sexual activity, with social conformity, and ultimately with death. In later chapters, Holden will see the tension between stasis and motion in terms of a succession of "falls"—all of them leading backward to the biblical Garden of Eden and man's Fall into the tragic condition of human experience. For now, however, Holden is simply casting about for alternatives to the life that brings a Stradlater and a Jane Gallagher into conjunction.

Thus, Holden ponders becoming a monk and living behind cloistered walls, where, as the poet John Milton once pointed out, *untested virtues thrive*. That is precisely the point, because what Holden imagines are saints who live above, or beyond, the world and who never engage in its messier battles. What authentic sainthood demands, however, is made of sterner stuff—not only because genuine piety is usually the result of great religious struggle but also because their lives are such models of selflessness and sacrifice that they cannot be measured by the usual human benchmarks.

In this regard, Holden is hardly a saint, much less a good candidate for monastic life. What his life does dramatize, however, is something of the same difficulty Holden has with potential roommates. In roughly the same way that he races to the conclusion that others are phonies, he insists that those who put away childish things inevitably become the enemies of purity. Holden, in a word, is a *prig*, a term that might be defined in the way that H. L. Mencken once described American Puritanism, namely, as the deep suspicion that somebody, somewhere is having a good time.

Meanwhile Holden keeps plucking the string marked *loneliness*, observing that an act as presumably simple as looking out a window can make one feel lonesome and even suicidal. Curiously enough, Huckleberry Finn often feels the same way and even uses many of the same images to express his isolation. In Holden's case, what he thinks about—once he returns to his room and the snoring Stradlater—are his fears that Jane Gallagher stood as little chance against Stradlater's wiles as he did against Stradlater's fists.

Jane *arrived* at that place on the other side of virginity where Holden pigeonholes those who are no longer "innocent." About this he is rigid, uncompromising, altogether priggish; and all without the slightest proof. Holden cannot *not* think about all that is lonely and sad-making and inextricably tied to Jane's innocence. But unlike Holden's penchant for disarmingly clear-eyed vision, this self-righteousness is much more a curse than it is a blessing. For just beneath Holden's inclinations to be either the fair knight in shining armor or Christ on the cross are wide streaks of the spoiled, the petulant, and the self-aggrandizing.

Consider, for example, Holden's parodic litany, his "stations of the Cross," as he prepares to leave Pencey: he packs his two, very expensive Gladstones (suitcases), including the new hockey skates his mother had sent a few days ago (he had wanted the *racing* type), counts up gift money from his grandmother (quite a "wad"), and sells his ninety-dollar typewriter for twenty bucks. For one who had earlier considered the monastic life, Holden is likely to have some considerable trouble with those orders that require a vow of poverty. He decides to get a hotel room in Manhattan for a few days and thus will be able to return home rested and ready to take on whatever grief his parents might dole out.

But that much said by way of Holden's plan, he is scarcely one to skulk silently away in the dark. What the moment requires is nothing less than a dramatic, ear-rattling exit—and as Holden describes the scene, one can see the various elements of his life at Pencey coming into conjunction: the paper-thin bravado that lies behind his efforts at sophisticated swearing, the strident nonconformity he associates with his red hunting cap, the oversized, dramatic way he announces his departure, the peanut shells that nearly spoil the moment by turning high drama into farce, and, most of all, the tears that result when one is, as he puts it, "sort of crying." We know better: nobody "sort of" cries, and as the factors that precipitate the tears become clear, Holden reaches the fraying ends of his prep school tether.

Of these elements, two deserve special mention as Holden's time at Pencey draws to a close: the tears that will ultimately well up and overflow in the book's concluding pages and the word "crazy," whose nuances will turn increasingly darker as he moves toward a physical and emotional breakdown. For those who refuse to accommodate, to *conform*, the world can be a scary, lonely place—as absurd and crazy as it is for Shakespeare's Hamlet and others who take up arms against their sea of troubles. But there are times when fighting against all that is rotten in Denmark, or in Pencey, is all that a good man can do. For Holden, the conformity demanded at Pencey may have set the stage and even arranged the props, but Manhattan is where Holden's drama of innocence and experience *really* unfolds.

A part of Holden really *does* want to go home, where his father may yell, and his mother may cry, but where both will soon start sending away for a new set of prep school catalogs. Moreover, home is where he can talk, really *talk*, to his sister Phoebe—because, unlike the assorted creeps at Pencey, she's no phony. What we watch is Holden's *ambivalence* and the way it plays itself out in the novel's subsequent chapters.

Small wonder, then, that driving through Central Park, he thinks once again about the ducks or that he asks the cab driver to have a drink with him at the Edmont Hotel. When it turns out that the cabbie doesn't share his concern about the ducks and that he hasn't time for a drink, Holden writes him off as yet another insensitive soul, but early in the game his bravado is wearing thin—and this well before he has felt the full force of what being down-and-out in Manhattan can mean.

Huck Finn floats down the Mississippi, in scenes that alternate between pastoral idyll and social threat, between those rare interludes when Jim and Huck loaf naked on the raft and those scarier moments when their raft is beset by steamboats or invaded by a pair of scoundrels named the duke and the king. Moreover, Twain makes sharp distinctions between nature and society, between the mighty river and the shore towns that sprang up along its banks. By contrast, Manhattan provides threats to innocence in abundance, but no comparable images of tranquillity—that is, unless one counts Holden's memories of the orderly, unchanging Museum of Natural History he used to visit as a child. For Holden, the museum has the smell of rainwater (even when it isn't raining outside) and gives one the sense that this is perhaps the world's only dry, cozy place.

Sadly enough, there is now no place where Holden is likely to find respite from the troubles that brought him to Manhattan, and this is certainly true of the Edmont Hotel. No sooner does he get into his downscale room than he finds himself looking out the window. No longer the suave, would-be sophisticate trying to order highballs, Holden simply reports what he sees with all the innocence of a country bumpkin out of his element in the big city: a cross-dresser in one case, and a man and a woman engaging in sex games in another. Holden freely admits that he watches all this with an odd fascination, but this is a case where curiosity does not a voyeur make. Rather, Holden's obsession with X-rated sexuality is a generous slice of his overall confusion. He doesn't understand sex, and in his most revealing moments, he readily admits this. Moreover, Salinger's novel provides ample evidence that *this* bit of self-analysis is right on target. One sees evidence in his ill-fated efforts to make a date with Faith Cavendish (an easy mark among the Princeton crowd); in his comic attempts to woo the three out-of-towners he meets in the Edmont's Lavender Room; and, saddest of all, in his encounter with the prostitute, Sunny, and her hairy-chested pimp, Maurice.

Holden is clearly much more comfortable as an observer of the city's tangled sexual mores than he is as a participant. Salinger is much more successful as a writer when he translates what Holden *sees* into vivid, memorable images. Consider, for example, this moment at Ernie's, a jazz club in the Village: a Joe College type, decked out in his requisite gray flannel suit and tattersall vest, is desperately trying to give his date an under-the-table feel. Both are more than a little drunk, and what Holden notices is that he is telling her about a person in his dormitory who gulped down a whole bottle of aspirin and nearly killed himself—this at the same time that his hands are busy, busy under the table. Meanwhile, the girl tries, in vain, to get her date to stop. The conjunction sickens Holden (as well it might anyone) and becomes yet another confor- mation of how lopsided and unjust the world, in fact, is.

In a novel that pits the phony against the authentic, the image of what is being said and what is being done—of the "story" told above the table and the fumbling seduction going on beneath it— reveals all that is required by way of learned, academic talk about the theme of illusion versus reality. Stradlater is destined to be- come one of the "very Joe Yale–looking guys" whom Holden feels almost *obliged* to hate, partly as a matter of overcompensation and partly because this is how smooth-talking, terribly *sincere*- sounding prep school Romeos end up. That a near-suicide and a clumsy effort at seduction can coexist strikes Holden as obscene (one can only concur in his judgment), but it is hardly uncommon. There are, as an old television show would have it, 8 million such stories in the "naked city" of New York.

Nor is it accidental that Holden's hypersensitive antennae fix on the small moment when sex-and-death are so intimately conjoined, for he equates sexuality itself with change, with mutability, and ultimately with death. That is why he is never quite in the mood to give Jane Gallagher a buzz and why he is so attracted to the unchanging character of the museum. Put another way, Holden is attracted to simplicity rather than to complication. He may talk a good game about the girls he has known, but one hardly needs to "read between the lines" to realize that he is as inexperienced as he is unsure about the opposite sex. Girls, in short, confuse him (what is he expected to do or not to do?). By contrast, places such as the Museum of Natural History are "natural."

Holden demands nothing less than the highest standards of purity—in motive, in execution, and, perhaps most of all, in "triumph"—or he rushes to the judgment that abject phoniness has yet again been at work. Consider, for example, the passages in which Holden tries to explain that even if he were to become a better lawyer than his father, one who devotes his life to saving the innocent, there would *still* be problems—because "even if you *did* go around saving guys' lives and all, how would you know if you did it because you really *wanted* to save guys' lives, or because you did it because what you really wanted to be was be a terrific lawyer, with everybody slapping you on the back and congratulating you in court when the goddam trial was over, the reporters and everybody, the way it is in the dirty movies? How would you know you weren't being a phony? The trouble is, you *wouldn't*" (172).

Small wonder, then, that Holden prefers his own (albeit, incorrect) version of "If a body catch a body." Indeed, *everything* about the aesthetic performance strikes Holden as right-headed and on the mark. For one thing, this kid walks on the street instead of the sidewalk; for another, he's involved with an interior game about walking a very straight line. Kids like that crack Holden up because what they do is so unpretentious, so uncalculated, so pure. Moreover, his song represents everything that Stradlater's whistling is not.

The song Holden mishears (Phoebe points out, correctly, that it derives from a poem by Robert Burns and that the first line is "If a body *meet* a body") is the occasion that generates Salinger's title and, later, Holden's most memorable speech, for his vision of standing "at the edge of some crazy cliff," as children play—innocently, without concern—in a rye field, is the novel's central image. Holden imagines himself as their savior and, given the image of Holden with his hands raised aloft, a good candidate for his self-appointed role as a surrogate Christ.

However, behind this striking image of Holden-as-Christ figure lies a complex network of contributing images: memories of his dead brother Allie, rotting unprotected in the ground; the fate of ducks during the unrelenting winter of Central Park; and, perhaps most of all, memories of James Castle, a fellow student at Elkton Hills who jumped to his death after unspeakable humiliations. Mr. Antolini covered the battered corpse with his sports coat (reminding us of Holden's earlier worry that he might jump to his own death and then lie on the pavement, uncovered, as people gawk at him); but nobody—not even Mr. Antolini—*caught* James Castle. He simply "fell" to his tragic, senseless death.

Even more damning, the well-meaning Mr. Antolini, Holden's favorite teacher, complicates an already complicated situation. Holden visits him in the Antolinis' swank Manhattan apartment (the couple is cultured, sophisticated, indeed everything that the Spencers were not) because he needs a warm bed and some tender loving (read: unconditional) care. What he doesn't want is a good talking to. But Mr. Antolini cannot resist handing out some badly needed advice, without realizing that the whole issue of getting Holden back on the straight-and-narrow academic track should probably wait until the boy loosens his grip of pristine dreams and begins the difficult task of engineering an accommodation with the world.

Therein lies the rub, for not only does Mr. Antolini quote psychiatrist William Stekel on the difference between the immature person and the mature one, but he also sends Holden into the cold sweats later that evening. Holden, now getting some much needed rest, awakens to find Mr. Antolini patting his head in ways that are, at the very least, suspicious. Was this a homosexual pass or simply the innocent gesture of a concerned adult who sees in Holden's adolescent confusions a reflection of his former self? Holden isn't sure, but he mumbles a series of unconvincing excuses and makes a quick exit.

Unfortunately, spooky thoughts and things pursue. For example, every time Holden steps off a curb, he thinks of himself as falling—down and down and down—as if to put teeth into Mr. Antolini's prophecy that he was headed for a "fall." But Holden's fall—unlike James Castle's or even the potential tumble of the children who play at the edge of cliffs—is not the sort that ends in broken bones and blood; rather, this fall risks an extinction of personality, a dissolving of the Self.

This dark feeling is linked to Holden's snap judgment about Mr. Antolini. Indeed, Holden now wonders (perhaps for the first time) if he might have been wrong. As he balances alternative interpretations (maybe he just liked to pat kids on the head; maybe he was a "flit," but, still, he had been very nice), we begin to watch Holden mature.

"Falls" continue to dominate Holden's consciousness as he makes his way toward his final meeting with Phoebe. Standing in Central Park amid a drenching rain, Holden watches Phoebe go round and round on the carousel. She is reaching for the brass ring, something that kids her age do, and Holden dearly wants to protect her from falling. However, he keeps his silence, realizing for the first time in the novel that you can't protect children from everything in the world, nor should you.

The novel itself concludes with Holden in a very different West from the one he fantasized about. As Holden puts it, "I got pretty run-down and had to come out here, and take it easy" (1). The *here* is a rest home not far from Hollywood, where his psychoanalyst wants to know if Holden will "apply" himself next September, at yet another new school. Not surprisingly, he cannot answer such a question, especially when so much of its weight rests on the slippery word "apply."

One thing, however, *is* clear—Holden, the narrator, no longer clings to the same desperate scenarios that defined him as a participant. Whatever lies ahead, it will not be a life as a saintly "catcher in the rye," nor will it include masquerades as a deaf-mute pumping gas in an ill-defined West. For better or worse, when the psychoanalyst rattles on about what his patient will be like next September, Holden listens and makes as honest an effort as he can to respond. He does *not* hand the doctor a blank piece of paper and a pencil.

More speculation than this is a mug's game, because characters, even ones as vividly rendered as Holden, do not outlive their last page. When Huck Finn finishes the final paragraph of his "adventures," he declares himself "rotten sorry" he had begun them in the first place. Holden also concludes on a note of sorrow but one that revolves around the idea that if you "tell" about people—even people like Stradlater and Maurice—you end up *missing* them, and in his farewell to them there is also the hint of an ambivalent farewell to a fondly remembered, but inextricably former, Self. Love does not come easily to the Holden who spares no pains when it comes to phonies; but there is a greater chance he will temper his righteous indignation than that he will fulfill Mr. Antolini's ominous prophecy about his railing against those who say "between he and I" long into middle age. Even more important perhaps, Holden's story—despite his regrets about telling it—makes good on Mr. Antolini's notion about the value of keeping a record of one's troubles and the way that the resulting work might help somebody who could learn from your experiences. Holden's voice continues to speak to those experiencing similar confusion, as well as to those who retain a fondness for him tucked somewhere inside their adult facades.

NOTE

Page numbers in parentheses refer to *The Catcher in the Rye* (Boston: Little, Brown, 1951).

STUDY QUESTIONS

1. *The Catcher in the Rye* starts with "If you really want to know about it," and employs the first-person narrative to tell the story. How would Holden's story have been affected if Salinger had employed a different style for conveying his ideas?

2. Salinger artfully captures many aspects of teenage culture of the late 1940s and early 1950s through Holden's dress and language. Yet, for many, Holden could also be a teenager today. Choose a scene and re-create it by updating the character's dress, language, and actions. Do you agree that Holden accurately represents teenagers of the 1990s? Are the problems Holden faces the same ones that teenagers encounter today?

3. Death as an image appears frequently in *The Catcher in the Rye*. Cite some examples of this image in the story and relate their importance to Holden's point of view.

4. Holden talks a lot about "phonies." Who would Holden consider to be "phonies" today? Who do you consider to be "phonies"? How does your list compare to Holden's?

5. Some people consider Holden the biggest "phony" in *The Catcher in the Rye*. Prepare an argument argeeing or disagreeing with that statement.

6. Critics often comment that *The Catcher in the Rye* raises issues that are universal and timeless. Explain how you agree or disagree with this point of view.

7. How important is Holden's socioeconomic status to the novel?

8. Much of the novel's action takes place in New York City. Describe how the novel would be changed if Holden spent the time after being expelled in some other setting.

9. Holden is a child of Manhattan. To get a clearer picture of what impact this has on him, compare growing up in Manhattan to where you grew up.

TOPICS FOR WRITTEN OR ORAL EXPLORATION

1. Write a paper comparing Holden as a retrospective first-person narrator with fictional characters who assume the role in other works such as *Moby-Dick*, *Adventures of Huckleberry Finn*, *The Great Gatsby*, or *The Invisible Man*.

2. Holden often refers to other works of literature throughout *The*

Catcher in the Rye. Write a paper that traces when and where those references occur in the novel. Discuss what roles the references play in helping the reader to understand the characters or action.

3. *The Catcher in the Rye* has been a controversial novel since its first publication and has often been banned from school libraries and courses. Prepare a defense of *The Catcher in the Rye* to present to your local school board.

4. We never get to see Holden's confrontation with his parents. Describe the scene as you think it would have occurred.

5. Holden is an "individual" in a time when bland conformity and materialistic values were the norm. Describe how you think Holden would fare in today's society.

6. Assume that you are Holden's friend. What advice would you give to him that would help him handle his problems with school, his parents, and girls?

7. Holden's brothers and sister seem to influence him a great deal. Compare his relationship with his siblings to sibling relationships from other works of literature.

8. *The Catcher in the Rye* was criticized for its obscene language. Discuss the importance of using this kind of language to tell stories. How important is the use of this type of language for telling Holden's story?

9. Some people criticize Holden's sense of morality; others laud it. Prepare a defense or condemnation of Holden as a moral character.

10. Discuss loneliness as a theme in *The Catcher in the Rye* in terms of Holden as well as other characters in the novel.

11. Holden mentions a lot of movies, even though he professes to "hate" them. Trace the use of these movies as a tool to help tell Holden's story.

12. Describe how Holden uses his theory of "phonies" to justify his failures.

13. Sports are frequent images in the novel. Discuss how and why Salinger employs this technique.

14. Write a comparison of the teachers mentioned in the novel to your teachers.

15. Write a comparison of the girls to whom Holden is attracted.

16. Holden considers himself an observer of life with a keen ability to pick out the "phonies." Write a paper analyzing this ability with specific examples from the novel.

17. Describe what actions you would take if Holden were your room-mate. How do you think Holden would rate you?

18. Compare and contrast Ackley to Stradlater as realistic characters.

19. Holden describes himself as "the most terrific liar you ever saw in your life." Carefully analyze this statement in terms of how "terrific" Holden's lies actually are and how important the lies are to the telling of his story.

20. Holden fails at many things in the novel, but not everyone agrees that he is a failure. Discuss the role that failing versus being a failure plays in shaping Holden's character.

21. Holden thinks of himself as a rebel when he describes how he wears his red hunting cap with its peak to the back. Compare Holden as a rebel with the teenage rebellions of the later 1950s and 1960s. How would Holden be considered today?

22. Discuss in writing whether Holden is the hero or antihero of *The Catcher in the Rye*.

23. *The Catcher in the Rye* depicts some of the social values that came to epitomize the 1950s. Write a paper describing those values.

24. There are some symbolic references to Holden as a "savior of inno-cents." Trace these references through the novel and analyze how well Holden fulfills this role.

25. Holden's attitudes about sex seem somewhat ambiguous. Discuss how these attitudes reflect the changing sexual mores of the post–World War II era. How would Holden's attitudes fit into today's moral code?

26. Phoebe is the youngest character in *The Catcher in the Rye*, and yet in some ways she is the wisest. Write a paper on the effectiveness of Phoebe's character for the novel.

SUGGESTED READINGS

Additional books by J. D. Salinger include the following:

Franny and Zooey. Boston: Little, Brown, 1961. *Nine Stories*. Boston: Little, Brown, 1953.

Raise High the Roofbeam, Carpenters and Seymour: An Introduction. Boston: Little, Brown, 1963.

Salinger's work has received a great deal of critical attention. The fol-lowing book-length studies are especially important:

Bloom, Harold, ed. *J. D. Salinger: Modern Critical Views*. New York: Chelsea House, 1987.

French, Warren. *J. D. Salinger*. Boston: Twayne, 1976.

————. *J. D. Salinger Revisited*. Boston: Twayne, 1988.

Gwynn, Frederick L., and Joseph Blotner. *The Fiction of J. D. Salinger*. Pittsburgh: University of Pittsburgh Press, 1958.

Hamilton, Kenneth. *J. D. Salinger: A Critical Essay*. Grand Rapids, Mich.: Eerdmans, 1967.

Lundquist, James. *J. D. Salinger*. New York: Ungar, 1979.

Miller, James E., Jr. *J. D. Salinger*. University of Minnesota Pamphlets on American Writers, no. 51. Minneapolis: University of Minnesota Press, 1965.

Pinsker, Sanford. *The Catcher in the Rye: Innocence under Pressure*. New York: Twayne, 1993.

Critical articles focusing on *The Catcher in the Rye* include the following:

McSweeney, Kerry. "Salinger Revisited." *Critical Quarterly* 20, no. 1 (spring 1978): 61–68.

Ohmann, Carol, and Richard Ohmann. "Reviewers, Critics, and *The Catcher in the Rye*." *Critical Inquiry* 3 (autumn 1976): 15–37.

Pinsker, Sanford. "*The Catcher in the Rye* and All: Is the Age of Formative Books Over?" *Georgia Review* 40 (1986): 953–67.

Rosen, Gerald. "A Retrospective Look at *The Catcher in the Rye*." *American Quarterly* 29 (winter 1977): 547–62.

2

Censorship of *The Catcher in the Rye*

The First Amendment to the U.S. Constitution seems to be clear in its intention to protect our freedom of speech. Yet, over the years there have been occasions when the people's right to speak freely or to have free access to the speech of others has been censored. One method this censorship takes is to restrain people from writing or speaking the words the public shouldn't hear. Another method is to limit the public's access to words that are already in existence. This chapter concentrates on the limitations or the attempts to limit access to *The Catcher in the Rye*.

The Catcher in the Rye has often been at the core of censorship controversies since its publication in 1951. *Catcher*'s main focus is the angst of teenage Holden Caulfield, which makes it a popular choice for inclusion in both high school and college literature classes. Because of this, most of the controversy involving the novel has been concerned with keeping the book out of the hands of students. Parents, ministers, school administrators, and, in a few cases, students themselves have challenged the novel.

The form that the censorship of *The Catcher in the Rye* has taken varies. In some cases its opponents want it removed as required reading in the curriculum. In some of those instances, merely allowing students an alternative reading choice has been acceptable. Some people who vehemently oppose the novel as *required* reading are perfectly content to have it as part of the course as long as it is only a *recommended* reading. Some school districts have settled the matter by restricting access to the book. They have parents sign permission forms before their students are permitted to read *The Catcher in the Rye*. Then there are those who are satisfied only if *The Catcher in the Rye* is banned from the curriculum of their districts. They want the novel off-limits for all students. At times, individuals or groups have felt so strongly about the novel that they not only want it kept away from minors but also want it kept away from all adults as well. The novel is often included on "dangerous"-book lists around the world. They want the book not only taken out of the classroom but also taken off the library and bookstore shelves.

The range of responses to *The Catcher in the Rye* involves many complex social, cultural, and religious issues. As we examine *The Catcher in the Rye* and the issue of censorship in the context of post–World War II culture we analyze why it elicits such strong feelings and what grounds opponents of the book use to support their points of view.

CRITICISM OF *THE CATCHER IN THE RYE*

Many of the challenges to *The Catcher in the Rye* condemned its use of profanity. Strong objections have been raised to the use of the four-letter obscenity that Holden finds written on the wall of Phoebe's school even though he is enraged to find the word on the wall and wants to remove it. There have also been objections because Holden flaunts the conventions of society. *The Catcher in the Rye* was published at a time when to be "different" was considered almost a crime. It's clear that Holden doesn't "fit in," although neither Holden's dress nor manner would set him apart from the crowd in our present culture. Even though the sexual references in *The Catcher in the Rye* can't compare to the graphic material in books, TV, and films available to children today, they caused the novel to be condemned across the nation.

EARLY REVIEWS

Despite the more than forty years of campaigns to ban the novel, most of the reviews of *The Catcher in the Rye* that were written when the book was published did not focus on the controversial issues that have kept it in the public eye. Some mentioned the language and sexuality, but these aspects of the novel didn't cause the furor in 1951 that they would in later years. The only criticism of those issues was based on how the language detracted from the literary style. James Stern so appreciated the novel that he wrote his July 15, 1951 review for the *New York Times* in a Holdenesque style. S. N. Behrman of *The New Yorker* magazine (where most of Salinger's earlier stories had been published) ended his August 11, 1951 review in "Holdenese" with "I loved *this* one. I mean it—I really did." Many of the other major reviews were also positive, recognizing the novel as a classic.

JOCELYN BROOKE (*New Statesman & Nation*, August 18, 1951): "[T]his is an odd, tragic and at times an appallingly funny book, with a taste of its own."

HARRISON SMITH (*Saturday Review of Literature*, July 14, 1951): "This is a book to be read thoughtfully and more than once."

PAUL ENGLE (*Chicago Sunday Tribune*, July 15, 1951): "Here is a novel about a 16 year old boy which is emotional without being sentimental, dramatic without being melodramatic, and honest without being simply obscene."

The July 16, 1951 issue of *Time* magazine ends its review, "He can understand an adolescent mind without displaying one." This is the gist of the differences between the positive and negative reviews of Salinger's novel. Many who didn't like the novel said the novel was adolescent, not just a story of an adolescent. This criticism also helps us to understand some of the complaints against it in terms of the censorship issues.

RILEY HUGHES (*Catholic World*, November 1951): "Not only do some of the events stretch probability, but Holden's character is iconoclast, a kind of latter-day Tom Sawyer or Huck Finn is made monotonous and phony by the formidably excessive use of amateur swearing and coarse language."

VIRGILIA PETERSON (*New York Herald Tribune Book Review*, July 15, 1951): "Recent war novels have accustomed us all to ugly words and images, but from the mouths of the very young and protected they sound peculiarly offensive. There is probably not one phrase in the whole book that Holden Caulfield would not have used upon occasion, but when they are piled upon each other in cumulative monotony, the ear refused to believe."

R. D. CHARQUES (*Spectator*, August 17, 1951): "Intelligent, humorous, acute and sympathetic in observation, the take is rather too formless to do quite the sort of thing it was evidently intended to do."

None of the reviews, no matter how negative, paved the way for the tumult that *Catcher* would cause for more than forty years.

CRITICAL REVIEWS

Most literary critics who write about *The Catcher in the Rye* concentrate on its literary merits, as the early reviewers did. Adam Moss reflected on the phenomenon of *The Catcher in the Rye* on its thirtieth birthday in *Esquire* magazine in December 1981. He also solicited opinions from a few of Salinger's colleagues, famous novelists in their own right.

FROM ADAM MOSS, "CATCHER COMES OF AGE"
(*Esquire*, December 1981)

ADAM MOSS

It might have been a fad, but it was not. *The Catcher in the Rye* became one of those rare books that influence one generation after another, causing each to claim it as its own. Today, in its fifty-third edition in the Bantam paperback alone, it sells almost as many copies as [it did] the first year it was published. . . . Now it is thirty and shows no signs of fatigue.

JOHN UPDIKE

I didn't read the book myself until 1955. Maybe I was already too old. I found it admirable—funny, poignant, vivid, actual—yet somehow less useful to my burgeoning sense of what writing was about than Salinger's short stories, which I had read in college. . . . I'm glad that *The Catcher in the Rye* has an enduring adolescent readership. That's a fine fate for it and makes it a very rare book.

PETER DeVRIES

Rereading it recently I found that I have an even stronger feeling of fondness for the characters than I remembered. It's a literature of character, really. Holden is a wonderful creation. Though he throws himself around as if he disparages the human race, he does not have the misanthropy that you associate with that kind of disparagement. He has a real *feeling* for people, that's the richness of his characterization. My guess is that it will last forever. Now, predicting something's immortality is a tricky thing, but then *The Catcher in the Rye* is a gem of a book.

TOM WOLFE

The Catcher in the Rye is a completely New York book. The cynicism about school and parents—that was completely alien to me. But the alien quality was also fascinating, as if someone had pulled back layers and revealed some strange and diseased terrain. Come to think of it, I doubt that I had ever met a real cynic prior to reading the book. Alien or not, though, it's one of the few books that artfully explore the doubts and humiliations that make up 95 percent of the life of an adolescent.

CRITICAL SUPPORT

The majority of the literary criticism on *The Catcher in the Rye* clearly classifies it as a work of art. Many of the writers, critics, and professors who write about literature feel there should be a "hands-off" policy where the arts are concerned. William Noble describes the response to a Moral Majority literary "hit list" written by librarian Gene Lanier from East Carolina State University in Greenville, North Carolina. When Lanier found out in 1981 that there would be a challenge to have a number of books, including *The Catcher in the Rye*, removed from library shelves, he mounted his own campaign. His theme, "A book is easier to burn than to explain," has been echoed in other efforts to stop censorship (Noble, *Bookbanning in America*, 120–21). Other academic and literary figures have spoken out to stop censorship. Often they highlight *The Catcher in the Rye* to show why they think the arts should be exempt from being censored.

FROM WAYNE C. BOOTH, "CENSORSHIP AND THE
VALUES OF FICTION"
(*The English Journal*, March 1964)

. . . a full catalog of [the protagonist's] virtues and good works would be unfair to the book, because it suggests a solemn kind of sermonizing very different form the special *Catcher* brand of affectionate comedy. But it is important to us in talking about possible censorship of the book to see its seeming immoralities in the context of Holden's deep morality. (162)

FROM FRANKLIN SCHLATTER, "*THE CATCHER IN THE RYE—*
WHAT ARE WE COUNTING?" IN *CELEBRATING
CENSORED BOOKS*
(Nicholas Karolides and Lee Burress, eds. Racine, Wisc.: Wisconsin
Council of Teachers of English, 1985)

The Catcher in the Rye is Holden's record of his troubles. Those who want to learn from the book will find there is much to be learned. But our learning will depend on what things we count and the reason for counting them. (27)

CHRONOLOGY OF EVENTS THAT INVOLVE *THE CATCHER IN THE RYE* AND CENSORSHIP ISSUES

The following are some of the cases where the controversy about the novel was made public and gained some national attention. A number of minor cases did not cause enough controversy for national media attention.

1951	publication of *The Catcher in the Rye*
1955	first attempts to ban *The Catcher in the Rye*
1957	banned in Australia
1960	banned in Louisville, Kentucky; teacher fired for requiring it
	Tulsa, Oklahoma, teacher reprimanded for requiring book
	dropped from the curriculum in San Jose, California
1961	public debate in Wisconsin over book
	Oklahoma City wholesalers attacked for carrying the book
1978	removed from the reading list of the Optional High School in Issaquah, Washington
1979	removed from the required reading list in Middleville, Michigan
1980	removed from school libraries of the Jackson–Milton District in North Jackson, Ohio
	removed from the school libraries in Morris, Manitoba
1982	removed from two high school libraries in Anniston, Alabama; later reinstated on a restricted basis
1983	challenged at the high school in Libby, Montana
1985	banned from Freeport High School English class in De Funiak Springs, Florida
1986	removed from the English class required reading list from senior high school in Medicine Bow, Wyoming
1987	banned from a required reading list for sophomores at the Napoleon, North Dakota, high school

1988	challenged at the high school in Linton-Stockton, Indiana
1989	banned from the high school in Boron, California
1991	challenged at the Community High School in Grayslake, Illinois
1992	challenged at Jamaica High School in Sidell, Illinois
	challenged in the Waterloo, Iowa, schools
	challenged in the public school libraries in Duval County, Florida
	challenged at the Cumberland Valley High School in Carlisle, Pennsylvania
1993	challenged as required reading for the Unified School District in Norco, California
1994	challenged at the high school in New Richmond, Wisconsin
	challenged in Goffstown, New Hampshire
1996	used to build a case by a student protesting censorship of a student publication
1997	challenged as required reading by a student in Brunswick, Georgia
	challenged as required reading in Marysville, California

ATTEMPTS TO CENSOR *CATCHER*

"You call yourself a Christian, but you're an atheist, a communist, and a smut peddler. Why do you insist on having children read four-letter words in school? Why do you want to fill their minds with trash? Why do you want to destroy America's children?" (Jenkinson, *Censors in the Classroom*, xi). Those words were in an unsigned letter received by Edward B. Jenkinson, teacher and author of a book on censorship, and show how heated the debate about censorship gets. *The Catcher in the Rye* was a popular and controversial book from its publication in 1951. There were no documented attempts to censor the novel until 1955. Once they started, however, they have continued for the last forty-six years. We will examine some of the attacks more closely. (See the full chronology of the attempts to censor Salinger's novel provided earlier in this chapter.)

An Associated Press news release, printed in the *New York Times* in March 1960, reported that a Louisville, Kentucky, high school English teacher was to be released from his contract after his current year because he wanted his tenth graders to read *The Catcher in the Rye*. The book was dropped from the reading list after the parents protested.

FROM ASSOCIATED PRESS NEWS RELEASE
(*New York Times*, March 1960)

Louisville, Ky., March 19 (AP)–A high-school teacher who put a controversial novel on the student reading list said yesterday school authorities were releasing him after the current year. Donald M. Fein, 30 years old, had proposed use of "The Catcher in the Rye" for male high-school tenth graders. The book by J. D. Salinger, is a frank study of adolescent life. It was dropped from the reading list after a number of parents protested.

That same year Mrs. Beatrice Levin, an English teacher at Edison High School in Tulsa, Oklahoma, was reprimanded by her principal for requiring her students to read the novel after eight parents complained. Mrs. Levin subsequently resigned.

In the spring of 1960 parents from the Eastside School District of San Jose, California, complained at a public meeting of the district's Board of Trustees about *The Catcher in the Rye*'s being recommended to some high school seniors. The parents felt that the novel was "unfit." Some parents at the meeting did voice concern that banning the novel was unwarranted, but it was dropped from the curriculum, and there were charges that the teacher involved was transferred to another school.

Groups such as the American Library Association (ALA) and the American Association of University Professors regularly supported the fight against censorship. In 1961, Lawrence Clark Powell, dean of the School of Library Service, Los Angeles, wrote a letter to the ALA Bulletin that *The Catcher in the Rye* needed to be defended more strongly. During the Wisconsin Free Library Commission's Eighth Institute on Public Management there was a move to support keeping the novel on library shelves.

During the same year wholesalers in Oklahoma City, Oklahoma, were attacked in a legislative hearing for carrying the paperback editions of *The Catcher in the Rye*. Supporters for banning this and a number of other books launched a campaign that included using a "smutmobile." They stopped at bookstores and newsstands all over the city in a vividly marked van with a loudspeaker system. If the business sold the offensive material, the news was broadcast. As a result the wholesalers dropped a dozen of the criticized titles, and they were no longer available in the area.

The social revolution of the 1960s didn't slow down the attempts to keep certain literature like *The Catcher in the Rye* from being read. The following three excerpts, all from 1968, exemplify the scope of the concern that was generated by Salinger's book. In January 1968, some parents of Grosse Point, the sophisticated and affluent suburb of Detroit, launched a campaign that was reported by the *Detroit News*. The second example of parental attempts to censor the book was printed in the Beloit, Wisconsin *News* and illustrates the influence mothers and fathers have over school boards. However, the parents' crusade is not always successful, as revealed by the third example.

FROM "*CATCHER* CATCHES IT IN G. P."
(*Detroit News*, October 10, 1968)

Catcher in the Rye took its lumps and its kudos at a meeting of the Grosse Point school board on 9 October before a crowd of 100 persons, and succeeded in retaining its place on a recommended reading list (5–1).

Major attacker was trustee Arnold P. Fuchs, a new-comer to the board, who said, "There are parts of this book I would not read aloud to you." On the defense was Board president Mrs. Alice Hykes: "My three children all graduated from Grosse Point High and read the book. It is well done, honest and not at all exaggerated. It probably is well on its way to becoming a classic in its field." School superintendent Theos I. Anderson noted that the book is on a list of books recommended for high school students by the American Library Association.

FROM "CRITERION: FILTH"
(*News* [Beloit, Wisconsin], March 27, 1968)

J. D. Salinger's *Catcher in the Rye* came under fire when the board of education for Joint School District number four met Tuesday night. Over 20 parents appeared at the meeting to object to several pieces of literature not required for Parkview's high school students.

One mother brought the Salinger book and a book of short stories that she considered objectionable and said her son told her they were on the school's recommended reading list.

Principal Edward Connors replied that the book is recommended by the American Library Association but is not on Parkview's list of recommended reading and only six of the nine short stories in question were used for classroom discussion.

One mother objected to the *Romeo and Juliet* film attended by students. Another mother said after she read Shakespeare she considered he "was a dirty old man" and added "I'll have the last say on what books my children read and what movies they see."

Connors said he had substituted for several books this year including John Steinbeck's *Of Mice and Men* and went on to say that 90 percent of the required reading list is the same as it has been for several years.

It was agreed to set up a committee of parents to work with teachers on the required reading list. Parents will judge their books not on their literary value but on what they consider "filth."

FROM "PASTOR PLEDGES FIGHT OVER *CATCHER*"
(UPI News Release, 1968)

A Baptist pastor said Monday he will continue to preach against the contents of J. D. Salinger's book *Catcher in the Rye* until public opinion forces school officials to remove it from suggested reading lists.

But school officials countered that the 17-year-old book is one of the standard studies of teenage turmoil, accepted nationwide by "reputable and conservative" library organizations. It has been in school libraries here for at least 10 years.

The Rev. Curtis Goldman, pastor of the Temple Baptist Church, said he, along with 36 members of his congregation, was willing to go to court to have the book banned from the Albuquerque Public School system.

The group met with Del Norte High School Principal John Hobeck Monday and demanded the book be taken off reading lists in English classes at the school.

"I don't feel the school officials will remedy the situation and I think public pressure will be the only solution," Rev. Goldman told UPI. He said he was willing to go to court to prove the book contributed to the delinquency of minors, was a violation of the Supreme Court ruling on religion in public schools and was discriminatory against persons opposed to books of this type.

Hobeck said the book is on the suggested, not required reading lists. He said one teacher at Del Norte had assigned the book, but he had told the teacher that alternate assignments should be made if a student objected to any book on moral grounds. He said no objections had been received. He said he felt no student should be forced to read the book if he feels it is objectionable, but he noted it had been in high school English courses for many years.

The following, from a series of articles in the Kansas City newspapers from January 18 to February 1, 1972, is a more detailed account of how one school district, Shawnee Mission South School District in Shawnee, Kansas, handled attempts to take *The Catcher in the Rye* off the district's approved reading list.

FROM "*CATCHER* CATCHES IT . . . AGAIN"
(*Kansas City Times*, January 18, 1972)

After receiving a three-page letter complaining about the use of *Catcher in the Rye* as a supplement to a sophomore literature class, the Shawnee

Mission Advisory Board voted unanimously to recommend to the school board to remove the book from the district's approved reading list. One advisory board member said the book must be eliminated because it has widened the generation gap and confused moral values within families. The complaint from an unidentified source said the book contains 860 obscenities.

According to the *Kansas City Star*, in its January 18, 1972 article, the matter was not on the agenda but arose on a motion from the floor, not from one of the board members. The action was taken after the board's chairman, David Schmidt, left the meeting. Schmidt, a school board member from the South area, said he had no knowledge that the subject would be brought up. He condemned his fellow advisory board members for taking the action in his absence. He said they "behaved like vigilantes and witch-hunters." He said he received more than fifty phone calls and letters, with only one in support of the board's action. He added, "I don't blame them for having opinions but when this type of action is taken, it is something else. We're not taking any book off our shelves. . . . We have to rely on our administrators, not self-appointed censors." A school spokesman said the district's news line, which normally handles 100 calls each day, had about 200 calls a day following the reported action. None of the callers condoned the advisory board's position.

The *Star* continued its story by reporting that South High School teachers called the recommendation "book banning." Jacqueline Musgrave, chairman, of South's English department, said, "The emphasis on obscenities is misleading. If students have not encountered the four-and-five-letter words before, they won't know what they mean. And that language is obsolete." Later, in that article, Norman Babcock, a district administration spokesman, said the book was used as a supplement for a literature program for high school sophomores. But one advisory board member said an English instructor had assigned the book to students as required reading. The advisory boards were created by the Kansas legislature to advise the elected school board on curriculum matters and other affairs. Advisory boards have no power by themselves, except to urge parents to know what their children are being taught. Babcock encouraged the advisory board to list the reasons it believes *Catcher in the Rye* should be removed from the district's supplementary reading list. Several members of the audience had shouted that many other literary and social studies books should be removed also.

The *Kansas City Star* continued its coverage of the story with the response to the school district's stand. Marilyn Mayberry, an advisory board member, then issued a public statement saying a great disservice had been done by erroneous reporting of its meeting. She explained that

> Mrs. Florence DuBois read a letter from a patron regarding objections to the book. Mrs. DuBois chose not to reveal the author of the letter or the teacher involved, with which I agreed. The advisory board voted to make a recommendation to the board of education regarding continuing classroom use of the book. Present classroom use removes the book from optional reading and places it on a required reading list. At no time was the word "ban" used and we did not suggest removal of the book from the libraries. A proposal, never moved or voted upon, was made to form a committee to study district materials and make recommendations. The vitriolic reaction to erroneous reporting on the meeting has been overwhelming.

Chairman Schmidt promised to place the matter at the top of the agenda of the advisory board's February 7 meeting. He added, "Each member will be given an opportunity to clarify his opinion and amend the minutes if he wishes." He said, "According to one reporter who worked on the story for the *Kansas City Star*, the board did make a formal recommendation. However, the minutes do not show this."

Several suggestions were received from other groups and individuals. A representative of People Dedicated to Quality (PDQ), with about 300 members, said, "We vigorously oppose the banning of any curriculum material as a result of pressures from individuals or special interest groups in the community. We of PDQ firmly believe the advisory boards provide a valuable function as public arenas for discussion and understanding of educational matters. We believe the professional staff, because of their specialized training and their professional integrity, is qualified to determine what should be included in the curriculum and when and how it should be taught."

The mother of a South High School student, Mrs. Clifford R. Putrier, said, "J. D. Salinger was an early supporter of sin. After his divorce, he became more and more withdrawn from society, proving he had not learned the lesson set down in his own book." She wondered if *The Catcher in the Rye* was the best book that could be placed on the required reading list. She added, "I'm not suggesting that students be restrained from reading the book, but it must be compared with other available books. If these opinions make me a witch-hunter, a vigilante, then so be it."

Berry Shalinsky, a high school student and president of the Interschool Congress, said the congress proposed that patrons suggest additional books with opposing views, not remove books from the curriculum. Commenting in a January 23 editorial on the reported banning, the *Star* said, "People who want to impose their personal beliefs on an entire community or tell others what they cannot read ought to be regarded with some caution. They mean well, they work very hard, and they can do a lot of damage." On February 1, the Shawnee Mission School Board voted against barring *The Catcher in the Rye* from the district's schools.

THE ATTACKS CONTINUE

In 1978 *The Catcher in the Rye* was removed from the reading list of the Optional High School in Issaquah, Washington. The campaign included a claim by a woman that she counted 785 "profanities" in the novel. "When a book has 222 'hells,' 27 'Chrissakes,' seven 'hornys' . . . then it shouldn't be in our public schools," she said. She claimed that the book brainwashes students and is "part of an overall Communist plot in which a lot of people are used and may not even be aware of it" (Foerstel, *Banned in the U.S.A.*, 146–47).

In 1980 *The Catcher in the Rye* was removed from the school libraries in Morris, Manitoba, for "excess vulgar language, sexual scenes, things concerning moral values." *The Catcher in the Rye* was banned from a required reading list for sophomores at the Napoleon, North Dakota, high school in 1987. Parents and the local Knights of Columbus complained about its profanity and sexual references. In 1988 *The Catcher in the Rye* was challenged because it was "blasphemous and undermines morality" at the high school in Linton-Stockton, Indiana.

We start to see some shift in the complaints in 1992, when *The Catcher in the Rye* was challenged because of "profanity, lurid passages about sex, and statements defamatory to minorities, God, women, and the disabled" in the public school libraries in Duval County, Florida. In 1993 it was challenged as required reading because it is "centered around negative activity" for the Unified School District in Norco, California. The book was retained, but teachers had alternatives available if students objected to reading the Salinger book.

In trying to condemn action taken against a student publication "Tongue," which was banned in 1996 from his school, Great Valley High School, Malvern, Pennsylvania, for being obscene, student Justin Leto refered to *The Catcher in the Rye*. He stated that although the novel uses "obscene" language and vulgarity, it is "praised and admired" and is even on the school's suggested reading list. He cited the often-quoted phrases and words to justify his argument. In this case *The Catcher in the Rye* is used as example to show the hypocrisy of the system.

CURRENT ATTACKS ON *CATCHER*

There might be a tendency to think that attacks against *The Catcher in the Rye* in our current society would be unlikely. But the following excerpts from the *Atlanta Constitution*, the *Sacramento Bee*, and the *Baltimore Sun* highlight the issues that remain at the heart of the controversy involving censorship and *The Catcher in the Rye*. The novel's current opponents represent a cross-section of the people who have attacked *Catcher* for more than forty years.

The *Atlanta Constitution*'s report focuses on the efforts of a sixteen-year-old student to have *Catcher* removed from the required reading list of her school. The student, Kimberly Gordon, like all students at Glynn Academy, can refuse to read any given book and may substitute another text for the assignment. The core of this debates rests on what right Gordon has to control what her fellow students read.

FROM JINGLE DAVIS, "CENSORSHIP OR CHOICE? CATCHER IN
THE SPOTLIGHT; BRUNSWICK GIRL WANTS SCHOOL TO TAKE
NOVEL OFF REQUIRED READING LIST"
(*Atlanta Constitution*, February 10, 1997)

Kimberly Gordon, a 16-year-old high school junior, believes she is as
qualified as anyone to judge the quality of J. D. Salinger's coming-of-age
novel, "The Catcher in the Rye."

"What makes those critics more qualified than I am?" said Gordon, an
honor student. "Just because a book wins awards doesn't mean it's the
highest and best."

The teenager is trying to have the book removed from the required
reading list at Glynn Academy, one of two public high schools here. She
objects to the book's sexual references and profane words—nearly 700,
by her count, all highlighted in yellow in her paperback copy.

"There's always somebody counting the bad words and missing the
point," said Matthew Freeman, senior vice president of People for the
American Way, a Washington, D.C.–based anticensorship group.

The Glynn County Board of Education is scheduled to vote tonight on
whether to retain "Catcher" on Glynn Academy's required reading list
for 11th-graders. They will hear presentations by Gordon—who stressed
that she is not attempting to have the book banned—and by educators
who are defending their right to select reading material for students.

School officials noted that Gordon could choose an alternate novel to
study if she and her parents, Kay and Jake Gordon, disapprove of
"Catcher."

Controversy over the 1951 Salinger novel is nothing new, Freeman
said.

"This is one of the most challenged books in American literature, in
part because it is a classic of American literature and it is in every public
and school library," he said.

Gordon has a right not to read Salinger's novel, Freeman said, "But
she has no right to subject her judgment of the book onto the school
system, other parents and students. The bottom line is that this is an
attempt at censorship."

According to data compiled by Freeman's organization, during the
1995–96 school year there were 475 recorded challenges to school materials nationwide, including 1 in Georgia.

Attempts to ban or restrict access to books in public schools have
sparked controversies in the metro Atlanta area over the years.

The book "Deenie" by Judy Blume, which includes frank discussions
of masturbation, menstruation and sexual intercourse, was banned from

Gwinnett County's public school libraries in 1986. It remains the only book widely banned in the area, although attempts have been made against others.

Pat Sandor, spokesman for the State Board of Education, said his office makes no attempt to regulate reading materials in the state's public schools, especially at a time when the system is turning over more control to individual school districts.

"It is a local decision," he said.

FROM WINDELL M. SMITH, "MOST CHALLENGED"
(*Atlanta Constitution*, February 10, 1997)

The books most frequently challenged in libraries around the country, ranked by number of challenges between 1982 and 1995.

1. "Of Mice and Men," John Steinbeck.
2. "The Catcher in the Rye," J. D. Salinger.
3. "Scary Stories to Tell in the Dark," Alvin Schwartz.
4. "The Chocolate War," Robert Cormier.
5. "More Scary Stories to Tell in the Dark," Alvin Schwartz.
6. "The Adventures of Huckleberry Finn," Mark Twain.
7. "I Know Why the Caged Bird Sings," Maya Angelou.
8. "Go Ask Alice," anonymous.
9. "Bridge to Terabithia," Katherine Paterson.
10. "The Witches," Roald Dahl.

Source: People for the American Way

FROM JINGLE DAVIS, "GLYNN BOARD VOTES TO KEEP CATCHER IN ITS CLASSROOMS"
(*Atlanta Constitution*, February 11, 1997)

The Glynn County Board of Education voted Monday night against removing "The Catcher in the Rye" from required and optional reading lists at the county's two public high schools, but left unsettled the question of whether it will be taught in classrooms here this year.

The board's action followed a protest filed by 11th-grader Kimberly Gordon, who objected to the J. D. Salinger novel's profanity and sexual references and asked that it be removed from the reading list at Glynn Academy High School because she believes it is without literary merit.

Under current policy, students who object to books on a school read-ing list are allowed to choose and study optional works on a one-to-one basis with a teacher. Such students are sent to the library during discussions of books they do not wish to read or discuss, a practice Gor-don said places her at a disadvantage academically.

Chester Taylor Jr., the board member who wanted the book dropped from reading lists, agreed with Gordon and pushed to ban classroom discussions of books deemed offensive by any student.

"No student should have to be sent out of the classroom because of an offensive book," he said. Taylor commented he also found the Salinger work devoid of literary merit.

Taylor's motion to drop the book failed 6–4.

Academy's English department [said] that the book [will] "continue to be used with the clear understanding that it is not required; there will always be options available."

Several board members, English teachers and School Superintendent David Mosely said they believed the word "required" does not preclude teaching of the book in classes this year.

The book "will not be taught to any student who objects and every effort better be made to accommodate that student," Mosely said. "But this is absolutely not a ban on teaching the book."

However, Taylor said he believes the English Department policy, which won board support, would preclude classroom teaching of any book if a student objects.

"I guess it will just have to be decided by a court of law," Taylor commented after the special hearing, which drew about 400 people, half of whom seemed to support Gordon's efforts.

Taylor and other board members supported the English department's recommendation that a consistent reading list for both county high schools be designed this summer. At present, Brunswick High does not include "Catcher" on its required reading list for 11th-graders.

Diana Cason, who teaches advanced placement classes and chairs the Glynn Academy English Department, recognized statewide as a depart-ment of excellence, said she believes the continued use of "Catcher" over the past 36 years indicates a "strong silent majority" is in favor of retain-ing the book.

Cason said removing books containing profanity from high school reading lists would eliminate "virtually every winner of the Nobel Prize for literature in the 20th century."

A parent leads the attack on *The Catcher in the Rye* reported in the the *Sacramento Bee*. However, the focus is the same as the censorship attempt reported in the *Atlanta Constitution*. In both cases, the novel's critics make a clear distinction between banning the book and taking it off the required reading list. The added dimension to this case is not only the condemnation of the novel for its sexual references and obscenities but also the condemnation of *Catcher* for its lack of quality as a piece of literature.

FROM CARLOS ALCALA, "CATCHER PULLED FROM COURSE,
NOT DISTRICT"
(*Sacramento Bee*, Metro final, May 2, 1997)

"The Catcher in the Rye" is not being completely banned in Marysville, but its academic role is in question.

In response to a parent who counted how many times the book used "Chrissakes," "damn," "puke" and other "profanities," the superintendent of the Marysville Joint Unified School District has pulled the 1951 classic by J. D. Salinger from the required curriculum.

"This is not an issue of book banning," said Superintendent Peter Pillsbury, who said district policy gave him the authority to pull the book.

The novel will be available to students, but no longer required, and its general use will be discussed. The district will set up a parent committee to review literature for school use, Pillsbury said.

The matter began last year when a Marysville High School junior came home and showed her parents the book she was assigned for American literature.

"She said, 'I think you better look at the book they want us to read,'" recalled Pam Souza, the girl's mother.

In response to initial complaints, several students were given a substitute book, Souza said. "The Red Badge of Courage," set in the Civil War, replaced "Catcher," the story of an angry high school dropout.

Souza stressed that she and her husband, Steve, were not trying to have the book banned, but felt American literature classes should study something else.

"We live in America. You can like garbage," she said. "We just felt there had to be better books out there."

The book's language and themes have made it a perennial target. One list of the 50 books most attacked between 1990 and 1992 had "Catcher" at No. 3.

Even so, the novel still sells approximately 250,000 copies a year. It is considered a literary classic and is widely taught as a realistic look at youth's disaffection with the grownup world.

Salinger's writing reputation is so great that it was considered major literary news when, earlier this year, it was revealed that one of his old magazine stories would be republished in book form.

All of this was of little note to Souza, who hopes to be on the parent committee.

"I don't think (Salinger) was respected," she said. "It's beyond me why it's been taught all these years."

FROM TIMOTHY MAY, "WHY HIGH SCHOOL STUDENTS SHOULD READ THE CLASSICS FIRST" (*Sacramento Bee*, Metro final, May 4, 1997)

I never thought I would find myself in agreement with the religious right about much of anything, much less the banning of a book assigned to local high school students. Yet on May 6, the governing board of the Marysville Joint Unified School District, will vote on whether to remove "The Catcher in the Rye" (New American Library, 1951) from its approved reading list, and I would urge them to go ahead and do just that.

Yes, of course I am against censorship in our schools and libraries. But I strongly believe that certain modern novels just do not work well on the high school level, and this is one of them. My criticisms have little in common with the objections raised by one Marysville parent concerning the book's subject matter and language.

"I want them to replace this book with something we can be proud of as Americans, with a representation of American literature," says Steve Souza in his letter to the Marysville school board. Apparently the tender sensibilities of Souza's 11th grade daughter were dealt quite a blow by the novel's language and action, a situation for which I must confess little sympathy. It seems to me the average 11th grader these days has heard stories and language that are far more shocking than those employed by J. D. Salinger. And contrary to this parent's opinion, this novel is indeed representative of the best of American literature, a subject I have been teaching on the high school and college level for the last 25 years.

Still, I agree the novel is a poor choice for most high school readers. I say this for literary, not moral reasons. Like many other modern novels, this work appears to be one that young people can "relate to" and understand. Relate to, yes. Understand, no. Unless students have some literary background—and believe me, students are short on background these days—they will erroneously see in the story of Holden Caulfield justification for youthful cynicism and existential angst. These are precisely the stances toward life that our culture needs to discourage, not promote—especially since these are the tired themes of our pop culture. Yet Salinger himself is conveying no such message; he is in fact presenting just the opposite to the perceptive reader. The story is told by an unreliable narrator and readers unfamiliar with modern literature's propensity for irony and indirection will just flat out misread the book.

All this is reason enough not to assign such modern works, at least not until students are familiar with the conventions and traditions of our literature—a familiarity that used to be more commonplace 30 years ago when "The Catcher in the Rye" and other modern works began appearing on high school reading lists. In the post-literate era of today, teachers are lucky to encounter a student who has read A. A. Milne or Roald Dahl, much less Twain or Irving or Hawthorne. Yet here we are assigning Salinger or George Orwell or Kurt Vonnegut or Alice Walker—complex modern novelists who tap into literary traditions that have been evolving since long before the appearance of the American secondary school and its misguided reading lists.

Those who feel inclined to rally to the defense of these modern high school favorites should have another think on the matter. If trends in the teaching of high school English indicate anything, they indicate how confusing the so-called "modern classics" have been for the average high school student, who upon graduation appears to adopt a lifelong disdain for similar literature, judging from the best-seller lists.

Back in the 50s, when English teachers first began straying from traditional works, the writer Flannery O'Connor criticized the trend. Few young people care for 19th century writing, she argued, because they of course prefer the explicit eroticism and visceral appeal found in modern storytelling. O'Connor was right:

> Students may not really understand modern literature, but the sex and violence certainly are interesting to them. Which is one reason the moral controversy arises: If students cannot resolve the emotional and intellectual difficulties presented by a modern work, how on Earth can they make sense of adult values in conflict—a plot device at the heart of most modern fiction?

High schools should return to the business of establishing intellectual foundations. Students should not be assigned modern novels until they have been introduced to earlier works and earlier traditions in coherent survey courses. Novels like "The Catcher in the Rye" should of course be available for students in the school library, but whether such works are assigned to bright 11th and 12th graders should depend on what courses the student has already completed. And teachers should select literature that promotes age-appropriate reading and thinking skills, not just literature that has received the blessings of high culture for the last 50 years.

"The first thing you'll probably want to know," begins Holden Caulfield in "The Catcher in the Rye," "is where I was born and what my lousy childhood was like and how my parents were occupied and all before they had me and all that David Copperfield kind of crap." The ironic allusion to Dickens—just like the confused and scared voice of the adolescent narrator—is rarely understood by today's younger readers. But if we assign Dickens and teach students how to read him, they will begin to gain the perspective they need to understand the intellectual and moral challenges presented by much of modern fiction.

So let's put Salinger back on the shelf and assign a classic. Students will learn more. And—who knows?—They may even acquire a taste for Hawthorne or Cather or Thoreau, not to mention the modern writers. In due time of course. All in due time.

Perhaps the best way to conclude the public response to the censorship of *The Catcher in the Rye* is to include an editorial from the January 17, 1998 issue of the *Baltimore Sun*. The superintendent of the Anne Arundel County Public Schools removed Maya Angelou's *I Know Why the Caged Bird Sings* from the ninth grade curriculum. The editor's response ties the present to the past in a telling way.

FROM "BEST METHOD FOR POPULARIZING BOOK IS TO BAN IT"
(*Baltimore Sun*, Final edition, January 17, 1998)

I can understand the concern of parents regarding a novel such as Maya Angelou's *I Know Why the Caged Bird Sings*. My generation had a similar controversy with the novel *Catcher in the Rye* by J. D. Salinger.

If you want to ensure a book will be read by every ninth-grader in the county, try removing it from the curriculum. Ninth-graders are a curious lot. I'm sure the school librarian will be busy ordering more copies to keep up with the explosion of interest in the banned novel.

With a little encouragement, maybe our young readers will actually be found discussing a novel outside of the classroom. Maybe some of the children will read other novels.

Most of my contemporaries will cite *Catcher in the Rye* as the novel that best searched out our junior high school consciousness.

Maybe this generation has to discover its own.

At first glance the issues addressed in the First Amendment— that there should be no law abridging the freedom of speech—

appear clear and simple. However, the attempts to censor *The Catcher in the Rye* show us that the issue of free speech is more complex. We cannot successfully analyze the attempts to censor J. D. Salinger's novel without looking at the entire censorship issue in its historical context.

HISTORICAL CONTEXT

Individual freedom, especially the people's right to speak or write what they want, is one of the basic tenets on which our country is founded. The men and women who lived in colonial America felt these natural and intrinsic rights were being infringed upon by the king and Parliament. Along with other reasons, they were willing to break all ties with the mother country and fight one of the greatest powers of the time to retain them. Thomas Jefferson wrote in the Declaration of Independence that there are some unalienable and God-given rights that no government can take away. These were identified as natural rights by the Enlightenment philosophers of the seventeenth century (Thomas Hobbes and John Locke) and those of the eighteenth century (Montesquieu and Voltaire). The Pennsylvania Charter of 1682 shows how seriously the colonists relied on these ideals. William Penn stated in his colonial charter, "Any government is free to the people under it where the laws rule and the people are a party to those laws."

These intellectual constructs have become an integral part of our American value system. The Massachusetts Body of Liberties was passed by the Massachusetts colonial legislature in 1641, where individual rights, including the freedom of speech, were first elaborated. During the Revolution the thirteen new states wrote constitutions that included declarations of individual rights; most specifically mentioned the freedom of speech. The first of these documents was the Virginia Constitution and Declaration of Rights in 1776. But Pennsylvania's Declaration of Rights was the only one to extend the freedom of speech and press to the people and not just to members of the state legislature. The first federal bill of rights was added to the Northwest Ordinance in 1787 to help govern any newly acquired territory of the United States.

Some of our early leaders worried that personal freedoms would not be protected sufficiently by the Constitution that was drafted between May and September 1789. There were long discussions about inclusion of individual rights, but the document was completed without them because the majority thought these rights were implied. However, there was difficulty ratifying the Constitution without an agreement to amend it with a list of well-defined individual rights. So those committed to ensuring personal freedoms insisted that individual rights be specifically delineated and added to the Constitution its first ten amendments or the Bill of Rights. Many feel the First Amendment to be the backbone of these rights. Even though the amendment appears clear at first glance, it has been the center of controversy in numerous areas.

Over the years some people have felt that the Constitution and the amendments—including those freedoms afforded us in the First Amendment—should be interpreted very narrowly. That means that the words mean exactly what they say, and no more. These people argue that the freedom to say and write what one wants should never be altered in any way. But, in practice, that has never been the case. The Constitution, and especially the Bill of Rights, has always been subject to interpretation. Freedom of speech in our country has always come with certain limitations. Sometimes those limitations are imposed by family, by religions, by society—and sometimes they are imposed by the law itself. Those limitations to our freedom of speech, no matter how logical or necessary, are censorship. Because people have their individual perceptions as to what should be censored and who should have the right to censor, the subject has always been controversial. When individuals or groups cannot agree what those limits should be, the courts have assumed the job of deciding which side is right.

The Supreme Court has taken on the responsibility to judge what is and what is not permitted by the Constitution. It retains the power to decide if laws abuse the rights of the citizens; and this is the same issue that the courts grapple with regarding censorship. They must weigh the rights of individual citizens against the responsibility of the government to protect the common good for the general population within the limits set by the Constitution. The specific case of *The Catcher in the Rye* has not been taken up by the Supreme Court; however, over the years, the Court has heard many cases that focused on the right to censor obscene and vulgar language versus the right to freedom of speech. The perceived obscenity and vulgarity in *Catcher* are the core of many attacks on it.

Throughout American history, there have been a number of notable cases that serve as landmarks helping us understand the broader issues involved in censorship. One of the most famous is the trial of John Peter Zenger in 1735 for seditious libel. He was prosecuted for making statements against the governor of New York, William Cosby. This case occurred more than forty years before we were a nation and more than fifty years before the First Amendment was written, but it set the precedent that if the printed information is true, it can't be considered libelous. The Zenger trial also emphasized that, as far back as colonial America, having the freedom to speak out—even if one directed remarks against the government—was important to the people. The key to the Zenger issue is the truth of the matter. Defamation is damaging another person's reputation by giving false information: slander is using speech to defame; and libel is using writing to defame. Although works of literature aren't usually attacked for libel, this aspect is at the heart of the censorship issue and helps to keep the public intent on protecting the right to free speech.

Censorship includes almost any situation that restricts the content or dissemination of information. One method of censorship is the government's use of "prior restraint," which is to stop a person or persons from communicating or to prevent an idea or ideas from being communicated. The Supreme Court has traditionally held that "any system of prior restraints of expression comes to this Court bearing a heavy presumption against its constitutional validity" (*Bantam Books, Inc., v. Sullivan*, 1963). Therefore, our system of government has traditionally held that there has to be an extremely valid reason to restrict speech on this basis. Prior restraint could stop an author from writing a book or article or stop a person from making certain statements. For example, Justice Oliver Wendell Holmes pronounced in his classic ruling that our freedom of speech does not allow us to yell "fire" in a crowded movie theater.

In cases involving the censorship of literature, as with *The Catcher in the Rye*, the courts are not usually dealing with the issue "prior restraint." Censoring literature means trying to keep people from having access to existing material because, for example, the work in question might be considered obscene, vulgar, or even dangerous. This has often been both an accepted practice and the subject of protests. Our culture supports the right of parents to stop their young children from coming in contact with material that they think is unacceptable. However, to do that means that parents sometimes try to have the material taken out of libraries or school curricula. This limits other people's access to the material, which, in turn, limits their rights. This is the central issue in the matter of this type of censorship: one side thinks that its First Amendment rights allow it to have access to the material, while the other side thinks that society is best served by denying people access to the material. The issue evolves into a legal one when the courts become involved and must decide whose rights should be protected. Although Salinger's novel has never itself been the subject of a Supreme Court case, the findings of the Court on similar cases have had an impact on how *The Catcher in the Rye* has been treated.

Other famous censorship cases have often hinged on the issue of protecting the public from information that is offensive. Opponents of *The Catcher in the Rye* often cite its offensiveness as the reason for wanting to censor it. Offensive means that the material is considered obscene or not up to the acceptable standards of society. This is a concept that is difficult to define legally. Supreme Court Justice Potter Stewart observed in what has become a famous quote, "I may not be able to define [obscenity], but I know it when I see it." The Supreme Court has in recent years allowed some community control over free speech by stating that the First Amendment does not protect all forms of expression. It has ruled that expression that has social value should be protected unless it causes substantial and demonstrable direct harm. Less valuable expression is "unprotected." It may be prohibited if the government simply shows a good reason to be concerned about its potential impact. Some writers, literary critics, educators, and social scientists argue that the story of Holden Caulfield has important social value and should be protected by our First Amendment rights. According to critic Donald P. Costello in "The Language of *The Catcher in the Rye*," an article for *American Speech*, "In coming decades, *The Catcher in the Rye* will be studied, I feel, not only as a literary work, but as an example of teenage vernacular in the 1950's" (340). Edward Corbett states in his article for *America*, "Raise High the Barriers, Censors," "Although in *The Catcher in the Rye*, the language is crude and obscene, some situations scandalous, and the protagonist guilty of the same phoniness for which he condemns others, this one novel that post-war young people read and discuss avidly really makes the older generation uncomfortable because it exposes so much of what is meretricious in our way of life" (104).

One of the earliest obscenity cases occurred in 1815 and involved a painting that the government of the young state of Pennsylvania thought was indecent. It was soon followed by a case involving a work of literature: *The Memoirs of a Woman of Pleasure* by John Cleland. Peter Holmes appeared before the Supreme Judicial Court of Massachusetts in 1821 to appeal his conviction for publishing the book in America. Cleland's novel had originally been published in England in 1748, at which time its author was imprisoned for writing lewd material, and the book itself was banned within eighteen months of publication. Holmes's conviction was upheld by that court, but despite the stricter moral codes of earlier times, few states enacted obscenity laws, and even fewer pursued them. It took more than seventy years until the next obscenity conviction in the United States. The heroine of Cleland's book was Fanny Hill, and it wasn't until 1966 that her story would be legally read by the general public in the United States. It is interesting that people in the United States would gain access to the affairs of Fanny Hill at about the same time some were forbidden to read about Holden Caulfield.

Besides restricting obscenities, we are also restricted in using defamation and "fighting words." Commercial speech, speech in special places, and speech that leads to illegal action are also limited. We know, for example, that it is against the law to even joke about hijacking an airplane, taking a bomb on an airplane, or threatening the president of the United States. In times of war, when our national security is threatened, freedom of speech has been limited even further. During these periods we are not allowed to say anything that would be considered a risk to our national security. Laws such as the sedition acts are passed to protect the country. Laws enacted during extreme national emergencies, such as during wars, usually cover very specific situations and time periods. They often have time limits to ensure going back to the original tenet of freedom of speech.

However, a few times in our history our First Amendment rights have been infringed upon without national security being threatened. These actions originated in specific historic eras when the political or social climate fostered an atmosphere open for some group to control the freedoms of others. The federal government of Adams's administration passed legislation to limit freedom of speech (the Sedition Act—June 18, 1798). The excuse was the quasi-war with France, but the actual motive was to stop the political opposition from the Democratic–Republican supporters of Thomas Jefferson. It was illegal to write, print, or say "any false, scandalous, and malicious" statement against the government or to "incite against them the hatred of the good people of the United States." It was never challenged before the Supreme Court because the Federalists were in control of the Court. It expired in March 1801 at the end of Adams's presidency. Jefferson pardoned the eleven convicted men when he took office.

There was a variety of issues involving the country and the censorship issue leading up to the Civil War. Individual antebellum southern states restricted free speech about slavery for both blacks and whites. To keep abolitionist literature from their populations, mail was censored. From 1830 to 1844, Congress refused to receive antislavery petitions but changed its policy because of public pressure. The restrictions that prohibited slaves from learning to read were a major infringement on First Amendment rights. Although the Supreme Court never addressed this issue directly, the Dred Scott case in 1857, which ruled that Dred Scott could not be a citizen, made this a moot point.

During the war a number of measures were taken to restrict freedoms. President Lincoln suspended the writ of habeas corpus in April 1861. The Supreme Court, led by Chief Justice Taney, invalidated the president's action in *Ex parte Merryman* in May 1861. Taney's Court ruled that only Congress could suspend the writ of habeas corpus. Lincoln justified his action by saying that he acted to uphold the law and couldn't wait for Congress to be assembled to act. In other cases Lincoln upheld First Amendment rights. General Burnside ordered the printing of the *Chicago Times*, which supported the South, suspended. Lincoln revoked the order.

After the war, workers tried to organize to gain better working conditions and wages in a movement that often became violent. Big business often had the power to curb the actions of the workers by forcing local governments to limit the workers' ability to have access to public meetings. The unions claimed that picketing was part of the freedom of expression, and that was often challenged by both the owners and the local governments. This issue would not be settled until the 1940 case of *Thornhill v. Alabama*.

Part of the South's resentment of Reconstruction was the establishment of antiblack groups like the Ku Klux Klan (KKK) and the Knights of the White Camilia. After Reconstruction ended in 1876, and northern troops left the South, these groups continued to flourish for a time as a way of controlling the former slave population. By the turn of the century most local and state governments instituted laws that also kept the blacks from attaining equal opportunities. The rights of black citizens, including those guaranteed by the First Amendment, were greatly infringed upon by legal, social, and terrorist means.

By the end of the nineteenth century the country was fully engaged in industrializing and urbanizing. The social fabric of America was changing, and there was a rising demand for reform. Obscenity became one of the reform issues, and soon the courts were involved with a variety of cases dealing with material that one segment of society wanted access to and another segment of society deemed unfit. These types of cases would be one of the foci of our courts for more than sixty years. *The Catcher in the Rye* was published in 1951, in the midst of this period, and has often been the focus of intense scrutiny. It has been banned from various school curricula and libraries for using obscene language and promoting unfit morals. We provide a chronology of *The Catcher in the Rye*'s involvement with censorship issues earlier in this chapter.

During World War I the Espionage Act was enacted to stop interference with the recruiting of soldiers or the draft and to prohibit anyone from "willfully [uttering, printing, writing, or publishing] any disloyal, profane, scurrilous, or abusive language about the form of government of the United States." More than 2,000 people were convicted of breaking this law. Challenges were heard by the Supreme Court, but the law was always upheld. The Sedition Act of World War I, which also restricted free speech, was also challenged in *Abrams v. United States*, but that, too, was upheld as constitutional. Eugene V. Debs was charged and later imprisoned for speaking out against the war. He was pardoned by President Harding in 1921.

Although the 1920s are often considered a period of social change, there were also aspects of the decade that harbored deep pockets of conservatism. During this period the infamous case of Sacco and Vanzetti occurred. Also during the 1920s the Ku Klux Klan was reborn and had millions of members from many of the forty-eight states. An act to set a quota on immigration was passed in 1924. Amid the glitter of the Roaring Twenties, elements of religious fundamentalism grew strong enough to gain power in some state and local governments. Some states tried to stop teachers from teaching certain material. The most famous case was the Scopes "monkey trial" (May 1925), in which the state of Tennessee took teacher John Scopes to trial for teaching the theories of Darwinism. We see a parallel to the censorship of *The Catcher in the Rye* because, in many cases, teachers were also censored and in some cases fired for using the novel in their classes.

A Red Scare also occurred during the 1920s. The period after World War I was dramatic for the United States: the fall of czarist Russia and the founding of the Soviet Union had a profound effect on the country. Many related the union movement that started in the mid-nineteenth century to socialism and anarchy and feared that the government could be overthrown by workers who supported socialism. They linked these movements to the eventual overthrow of the U.S. government, especially after the formation of the Communist Party in Chicago in August 1919. The fear was enflamed by the growing labor movement and a number of strikes that occurred after the war, when the economy was in a slump. A. Mitchell Palmer, the attorney general, spearheaded a drive to "protect" the country from the "Red Menace." In one night alone there were 4,000 arrests all over the country of people who were considered dangerous because of what they thought, wrote, or said.

The fear of communism is the focus and rationale for censorship after the 1920s. The Dies Committee investigated subversive propaganda in the 1930s. This House committee was the precursor to the House Un-American Activities Committee (HUAC), the committee that investigated activities it deemed un-American. In 1939 they investigated material in a series of social science textbooks by Professor Harold C. Rugg as being anti-American business. The business community argued that the texts were a threat to capitalism because they prompted citizens to question the effectiveness and safety of American products. B. C. Forbes, the editor of *Forbes* magazine, led an attack on the textbooks being used by the Englewood, New Jersey, School District as well as by a number of other districts across the country. Forbes was joined by a council representing more than forty patriotic groups. The Daughters of the American Revolution, the Advertising Federation, and the American Legion all mounted campaigns to force school districts to drop the textbooks. This had the reverse effect on the sales of the book, and by 1940 more than 5,000 local school districts were using the books. The attacks continued, despite support from a number of prominent publishers, authors, clergymen, and college professors, such as Bennett Cerf, W. W. Norton, and Fannie Hurst. The controversy heated up so much that Rugg's books were actually burned in Ohio. Patriotic groups expanded their crusade to have the political views of other social science authors cataloged to keep the nation protected from unpatriotic (liberal) views. There was even some effort to have all social studies courses banned from school curricula. A major confrontation was avoided only because the United States was attacked at Pearl Harbor and entered World War II, when most liberal views were overshadowed by support of the war. Although obscene material was not at the center of this effort by one group of citizens to control other groups' access to the written word, it set the stage for the postwar era, when books such as *The Catcher in the Rye* came under the scrutiny of various groups.

By the 1940s most laws enacted by the federal government dealing with censorship focused on national security. In 1940 the Smith Act (H.R. 5138) made it a crime to teach or advocate the violent overthrow of the U.S. government and was called the "omnibus gag bill" by those who opposed it. Under this law, antiwar or antimilitary literature was often prosecuted. The Walsh Bill made it a crime to publish a book that would seem to advocate that a member of the armed forces disobey an order. It also made it legal to confiscate any printed matter from a dwelling without a search warrant. The conservative Right as well as the liberal Left were controlled by acts such as these. In 1941 the government took action against Father Coughlin's pro-Nazi *Social Justice* magazine and Robert Wood, the owner of the Progressive Bookstore in Oklahoma City who was a member of the Communist Party.

Once World War II began, the federal government began to take a more active role in censorship. An Office of Censorship was set up with Byron Price, a former head of the Associated Press, as its chief. In reality, the rules it made tried to allow the press and publishers the greatest amount of freedom under the circumstances. For the most part, they left the decisions of what should be published up to the discretion of those who published the material. The government let "common sense" prevail, with the understanding that nothing would be printed that could aid the enemy. Overall, the relationship worked well, with the providers policing themselves to help with the war effort. But there was still public pressure to control the moral values of America. This pressure ignited after the war inflaming many to protect the public from books like *The Catcher in the Rye* that they considered obscene. The post office even used wartime censorship standards to try to keep material it deemed unfit out of the mail. But in 1943 the Supreme Court issued an opinion that the U.S. Post Office did not have the right to decide what was fit to be sent through the mail. This decision was based on a case against *Esquire* magazine. The post office also tried to keep a book of songs by and for men in service out of the mail because the post office thought it was obscene but decided to drop the issue because of public pressure. Religious and patriotic groups continued to try to control the material to which the armed forces had access. The result was an amendment to the 1944 Soldiers' Vote Bill that gave the government the power to censor literature sent to members of the armed forces. Public pressure forced the passing of another amendment that canceled the first.

On the whole, most of the efforts to control or censor literature came from specific power groups and were aimed at specific targets rather than from the federal government. In some states the business community had the power to go after opponents, usually those they felt had "communist" or "liberal" leanings. This usually meant anyone who advocated the right for the consumer to hold business accountable. In other states the Catholic Church had the power to attack any publications it thought were corrupting the morals of society. The religious element was concerned with literature that was both obscene and too liberal. This element attacked any publications that it thought might pull people from the Church. Some state governments themselves took an active role in trying to censor citizens' access to literature. This was especially true in the South, where states such as Georgia kept books—both texts and fiction—from the schools and libraries if they promoted or seemed to promote civil rights. In some states the local government had the control. In Boston the police had the power under the criminal code to confiscate books it felt were unfit (usually for being too sexually explicit) from stores. Boston and the state of Massachusetts had long held very strict moral codes for what was considered proper for public consumption. The term "banned in Boston" was often used to describe literature thought to be too "sexual," such as *Ulysses, Lady Chatterly's Lover*, and *Forever Amber*. Had *The Catcher in the Rye* been published then, it probably would have been included on this list. Groups such as these solidified their efforts in the postwar era.

Much of the censorship issue during the postwar period dealt with limits on our First Amendment rights for political reasons that were linked to the Cold War and the fear of communism's threat of world domination. A number of laws were passed to stop the spread of communism. Broad powers were given to those on the local, state, and federal level to interpret those laws and protect society. These powers included not only what people could say and write but also, in some cases, what they might think or feel. The people in power, such as Senator McCarthy, didn't need proof to accuse someone of being a communist. There wasn't even the need for a trial. Accusations alone were enough for people to be blacklisted and ruined.

The atmosphere of the 1950s also fostered growing constraints on other aspects of American society. The 1950s was a time of conformity, as we will show in a later chapter. It didn't pay to be different or too controversial. Books that were published during this period were often targeted for attack. *The Catcher in the Rye* falls into this category. Books with neither the profanity nor the sexual reference that *Catcher* has were attacked as well. These books include *Raintree County, The Diary of Anne Frank*, and *A Diary of Love*. Representatives of one Ohio town's council wrote to a distributor that they considered "almost all" paperback books to be obscene.

The second half of the 1950s saw a number of Supreme Court cases that finally began to loosen the restrictions placed on literature. A landmark case in 1957 against Samuel Roth for publishing obscene material set new standards. The ruling stated that the government could take action to suppress a book only if it did not have any merit as "literature." That meant that if the work had any value at all for society as a work of art, that value weighed more heavily than the problems it could cause the government or the society. The Court finally decided that not all sexual matter was obscene.

The 1960s continued to be a pivotal time for the courts and the obscenity issue. The changes occurring in society such as the Civil Rights movement and the Vietman War had a far-reaching effect on what the courts interpreted as obscene. Yet, throughout the 1960s and into the present time, books continued to be censored, banned, or otherwise restricted by individuals, religious groups, or local governments. How and what literature is considered obscene and what rights the society had to control the public's access to that literature have evolved since the late 1950s. By the mid-1960s the Supreme Court no longer focused on what society, the lower courts, or legislatures had considered obscene. This did not entirely settle the issue. There were still cases in the 1960s involving people such as Ralph Guinzburg, who was jailed for distributing his magazine *Eros*, or Lenny Bruce, the famous comic who was constantly in trouble for his use of four-letter words. But, by the mid-1960s Americans could read books like Henry Miller's *Tropic of Cancer* or John Cleland's *Fanny Hill* for the first time. The only qualifications the Court put on First Amendment rights were where children were concerned. The courts did and still do feel that society has the right to control what its children can or cannot read. Many works of literature have been kept out of our schools for being too erotic or for using foul language. Examples include James Joyce's *Ulysses*, D. H. Lawrence's *Lady Chatterley's Lover*, and J. D. Salinger's *The Catcher in the Rye*. We are also now seeing efforts to keep books away from our children because they are accused of representing "racist stereotypes" (Mark Twain's *Adventures of Huckleberry Finn*) or of not representing correct "family values" (Toni Morrison's *The Bluest Eye*).

The results of the Commission on Obscenity—a panel of experts convened by Lyndon Johnson in 1967—concluded in 1970 that there was no evidence that viewing obscene material had any negative effect on adults. President Nixon rejected the findings. The Supreme Court also rejected them in 1973 in three landmark cases that again redefined the basic test for obscenity from its last major finding, the Roth case in 1957. The major difference in the findings of the Warren Court of the 1950s and the Burger Court of the 1970s was who was to decide what standards would be used to define obscenity. The Burger Court found that local, not national, standards should be used to determine what was obscene. In 1973 the Supreme Court decreed in the case of *Miller v. California* that speech or conduct is obscene if it has all the following characteristics:

1. An average person using the standards of the community would find the work, taken as a whole, to be obsessively interested in sex.
2. Sexual conduct that is prohibited by law is depicted by the work.
3. There is no serious literary, artistic, political or scientific value to the work.

Another change from the 1957 decision was that the burden of proof shifted. It became the responsibility of those who wanted access to a work to prove that it had "redeeming" value for society. This was a drastic change from the Roth verdict, which said that the work could not be banned if it had any artistic value at all. Yet, the impact of this decision was minimal. We did not see a new rash of book burning or police raids to keep books from the public, because the social and sexual revolutions of the 1960s had some effect on people's attitudes. As the 1970s progressed, the liberal trends of the 1960s, the failure of the Vietnam War, and the repercussion of the Watergate scandal helped to start a conservative backlash. The "Silent Majority" stopped being silent and became a very vocal "Moral Majority." Since the courts gave the power to decide the moral limits to local communities, members of this group began to organize.

A number of issues in the 1970s had political implications, like the effort by the government to suppress the printing of the Pentagon Papers by the *New York Times* and *Washington Post* in 1971. This became a landmark decision and emphasized the perceived abuses of the government during the volatile period of the Vietnam War. In 1977 First Amendment rights were again an issue when neo-Nazis wanted to march through Skokie, Illinois, a town with a large population of Holocaust survivors. The American Civil Liberties Union defended them by saying their rights had to be protected as "the price we pay for liberty."

During the decade of the 1980s, a renewed interest in family values and a return by many to a more fundamental approach to religion stimulated more desire to control access to material that might be considered obscene by one segment of the population. The Moral Majority not only gained more social support but also became more politically organized. The conservative concerns about obscenity continued and expanded to areas like television and computers. By the mid-1990s the v-chip and laws to control the Internet became topics of interest.

LEGAL FOUNDATIONS FOR LIMITS TO
FREEDOM OF SPEECH

Although censorship of literature is our central concern because of its impact on *The Catcher in the Rye*, the topic has a much more far-reaching interest for students today. Few teenagers are unaware of efforts of people, including Tipper Gore, to censor song lyrics or of the pressure by many parents and religious groups to control movies and television. The newest efforts to control access to material involves trying to limit what is available on the Internet. We will, therefore, provide a comprehensive chronology of all types of Supreme Court cases with censorship as the central issue to be decided. We also include a brief historical perspective of the events and time periods that fostered the most intense censorship efforts.

The Supreme Court rules on cases based on the following issues concerning freedom of speech:

1. *Symbolic speech or speech plus*—The Court has had to decide in a number of cases what exactly "speech" means. They have included a number of forms of expression, such as flag burning and picketing. In most cases the Court makes the distinction between speech and actions. Speech is often protected even when action is regulated. The basis for rulings in these cases is whether the action conveys a message in itself without needing words. This a difficult distinction to make, and the Court must consider a wide variety of issues when assessing these cases.

2. *Public forum*—The government must not only protect an individual's right to speak but also protect that individual's right to have a public forum to express those views. The Court has ruled, however, that although the government may not deny the right, it can regulate the "time, place, and manner" it may occur.

3. *Over breadth and vagueness*—The Court makes sure that laws restricting speech are specific to ensure against the government having too much power.

4. *The right not to speak*—Just as the government can't keep a person from speaking, the Court has also ruled that the government can't force a person to speak. This is most apparent in cases involving the Pledge of Allegiance.

5. *The government as speaker*—The Court has also ruled that the government has a right to have point of view and to promote that point of view.

6. *Obscenity*—The Court deals with cases to judge which information should be kept from the people. The material that violates society's standard of decency is usually found to be obscene.

7. *Defamation*—The Court usually finds that untruthful written or spoken statements are not protected under the First Amendment.

8. *Fighting words*—Abusive or insulting language known as "fighting words" is not protected as First Amendment rights.

9. *Commercial speech*—Commercial speech such as advertising may be regulated and therefore is not fully protected.

10. *Speech in special places*—Restriction of speech may apply in some places even if it would normally be protected. Those places include prisons, schools, and army bases.

11. *Speech that leads to illegal action*—This issue has been difficult for the Court. It is easy to see with this issue how the times influence the decisions of the Court. At times there had to be "a clear and present danger" to the nation for the Court to restrict speech. At present the speech must lead directly to incite specific and unlawful acts to be restricted.

The Court has, however, heard cases the laid the foundations for arguments on both sides of the issue of censorship. The following chronology lists the major Supreme Court cases involving censorship. It is important to note the evolution of the findings of these cases.

CHRONOLOGY OF LANDMARK SUPREME COURT CENSORSHIP CASES

1821	Peter Holmes is tried for obscenity for publishing *The Memoirs of a Woman of Pleasure*. The conviction is upheld by the Supreme Judicial Court of Massachusetts. The book was banned until 1966.
1915	The Court ruled that moving pictures are not the press. Pictures have to be acceptable to the standards of the community (see 1952).

1919   *Schenck v. United States*—conviction upheld for mailing pamphlets to resist the draft. Holmes: "Words can be weapons . . . the question in every case is whether the words are used in such circumstances and are of such a nature as to create a clear and present danger that they will bring about the substantive evils that Congress has a right to prevent."

1925   *Gitlow v. New York*—Gitlow, a socialist, was accused under a New York law of inciting revolution by publishing a pamphlet. He said the law was unconstitutional because his First Amendment rights couldn't be taken away by a state law. New York won.

1931   *Near v. Minnesota*—newspaper banned as public nuisance as a prior restraint. Near won.

1938   *Lovell v. Griffin*—city manager controls what literature is distributed. City lost.

1940   *Thornhill v. Alabama*—speech and action—Court upheld that peaceful picketing was protected.

1942   *Chaplinsky v. New Hampshire*—Chaplinsky called official "damned fascist." He lost.

1943   *West Virginia State Board of Ed. v. Bernette*—students (in this case Jehovah's Witnesses) can't be forced to say the Pledge. Bernette won. This overturned the 1940 case *Minersville School District v. Gobitis.*

1946   *Hannegan v. Esquire, Inc.*—postmaster wanted to revoke *Esquire*'s second-class mailing privileges because it was not serving the public good. *Esquire* won.

1951   *Joseph Burstyn, Inc. v. Wilson*—New York wanted to ban motion pictures it found "sacrilegious." New York lost.

1951   *Dennis v. the United States*—upheld the Smith Act.

1952   The Court extended First Amendment rights to motion pictures.

1953   *Cox v. New Hampshire*—the Court ruled that the time, place, and manner of speech can be limited if content is not involved.

1957   *Yates v. the United States* limited Smith Act—government can punish an action, not a belief.

1957   *Roth v. United States* and *Alberts v. California*—the Court deals with obscene material that, for the most part, has not been a Concern of the Court. It continued to support the idea that state and federal laws on the topic were constitutional and therefore not protected under the First Amendment.

1964   *New York Times v. Sultan*—made libel harder to prove when public officials are involved.

1965   *Freedman v. Maryland*—allowed government censorship of obscene movies but only if stringent procedures are followed, including prompt judicial review.

1969   *Stanley v. Georgia*—the Court upholds the right to possess obscene material in the privacy of one's home.

1969   *Tinker v. Des Moines School District*—students wore black armbands to protest the Vietnam War despite a school rule and were suspended. The students claimed their freedom of expression was being censored. The students won the right to wear the armbands.

1969   *Brandenberg v. Ohio*—KKK conviction overturned—speech has to advocate imminent action.

1969   *Red Lion Broadcasting v. FCC*—"Of all forms of communication, it is broadcasting that has received the most limited First Amendment protection." Upheld the power of the Federal Communications Commission (FCC) to regulate more than newspapers.

1971   *New York Times v. the United States*—government used prior restraint (for first time successfully) to stop the publication of the Pentagon Papers. *Times* won. Justice Hugo Black: "In the First Amendment, the [Founders] gave the free press the protection it must have to fulfill its essential role in our democracy. The press was to serve the governed, not the governors."

1971   *Cohen v. California*—some obscene speech may be used for political statements to express intense emotions.

1972   *Branzburg v. Hayes*—reporters must answer questions.

1973   *Miller v. California*—the Court ruled there is a three-part test to prove obscenity. It gave power to communities.

1976	*Nebraska Press Association v. Stuart*—journalists couldn't be prohibited from publishing material potentially prejudicial to a criminal defendant if the material had been obtained in open court.
1976	*Buckley v. Valeo*—no limits to how much someone can spend on a candidate.
1977	*Wooley v. Maynard*—an individual can't put "live free or die" on license plate.
1980	*Snepp v. United States*—government employees may have their speech and writings censored even after they leave their jobs. Permissible prior restraint (CIA). (Snepp worked for the Central Intelligence Agency [CIA] and wanted to publish his memoirs after he left the agency.)
1988	*Bethel School District v. Fraser School*—students don't have the same rights as adults.
1988	*Hazelwood School District v. Kuhlmeier*—granted public elementary and secondary school broad power to censor student publications. "Educators do not offend the First Amendment by exercising editorial control over the style and content of student speech in school-sponsored expressive activities so long as their actions are reasonably related to legitimate pedagogical concerns."
1989	*Texas v. Johnson*—flag burning was symbolic speech. The Court ruled that the government may not prohibit the expression of an idea simply because society doesn't like it.
1990	*United States v. Eichman*—protesters burned flag on the steps of the Capitol to protest Flag Protection Act. The Court found act to be unconstitutional.
1991	*Rust v. Sullivan*—planning clinics can limit talk of abortion.

STUDY QUESTIONS

1. Some of the specific complaints about *The Catcher in the Rye* stem from its use of profanity, like the words written on the walls of Phoebe's school. Develop the policy for your school district concerning literature containing these kinds of words. Justify at which age, if any, your district should allow students to be exposed to such language.

2. Salinger conveys the message of *The Catcher in the Rye* through a specifically chosen language. Analyze the importance of the passage where Holden sees the foul language written on the walls at Phoebe's school. Discuss other methods Salinger could have employed to get his point across.

3. Holden uses profanity often in the novel. Discuss why you think Salinger has Holden use this type of language. Explain if you think it is necessary for the development of the plot or characters.

4. Imagine that *The Catcher in the Rye* was the subject of a Supreme Court case. Parents have used public opinion to force the local high school to remove the novel from the school library. Research previous rulings of the Supreme Court to cite in your argument. If you represent the side that wants the book banned, which information will help and which will hurt your case? How would your case change if the parents just wanted the book taken off the required class reading list or dropped from the course curriculum?

5. Describe how a "strict interpretation" of the Constitution would affect the public's ability to censor books like *The Catcher in the Rye*.

6. Use other works of literature that you have had in school and rate *The Catcher in the Rye* for being offensive and obscene. Explain your rating system.

7. Some people want to limit access to the Internet because obscene information is available to children. Compare the arguments for this issue with arguments given about *The Catcher in the Rye*.

8. Research the 1960 cases from the chronology of censorship issues and *The Catcher in the Rye*. Prepare an article for your school newspaper supporting or defending the teachers as you would have written it in 1960. Rewrite the article as if the censorship issue arose today; use the 1960 cases as historical references. What other material could you add to support your argument?

9. Censorship of *The Catcher in the Rye* usually centers on the vulgarity of the language or the sexual exploits in the book. Compare the arguments for the two issues and assess their validity.

10. Refer to Chapter 3 to see what, if any, impact the social context of the times had on why *The Catcher in the Rye* was censored.

11. *Miller v. California* sets three standards to determine if conduct or speech is obscene. Use those standards to judge *The Catcher in the Rye*. Write an opinion based on those standards.

12. In March 1997 the Supreme Court made its ruling on censorship on the Internet. Research this ruling and compare it to campaigning to censor *The Catcher in the Rye*.

TOPICS FOR WRITTEN OR ORAL EXPLORATION

1. Trace the origins of the First Amendment through events that occurred during the colonial period. Show how specific happenings planted seeds for protecting our freedom of speech.

2. The First Amendment states that Congress "shall make no law prohibiting the free exercise thereof; or abridging the freedom of speech." There are, however laws that do limit speech. Write a paper that evaluates the laws made by Congress and their compatibility with the First Amendment.

3. Research your school district's censorship policy as if you were preparing a series of newspaper articles on the subject. The first article should include any history of censorship in your district. The second should be an in-depth coverage of the current policy. The final article should include the response of people in the district, including students, teachers, parents, and other residents.

4. The trial of John Peter Zenger in 1735 is often cited as the root of the censorship issue in the United States. Compare and contrast the issues in this case with the censorship issues involving *The Catcher in the Rye*.

5. Even though Justice Oliver Wendell Holmes ruled that freedom of speech does not give us the right to yell "fire" in a crowded theater, the Supreme Court has been very guarded in supporting most forms of prior restraint. Research the instances when the Court dealt with this matter. Prepare a persuasive argument to support or condemn the use of prior restraint of speech in the United States.

6. The young government of the United States tried to limit speech for some of its citizens shortly after the ratification of the Bill of Rights with the passage of the Alien and Sedition Acts in 1798. Research these laws and the Supreme Court of the period. Imagine that a suit against these acts was heard before the Supreme Court. Prepare both the majority and minority opinions you think the Court would hand down.

7. Prior restraint is often enforced during wars when our national security is threatened. Compare censorship in World Wars I and II with censorship in the Vietnam War. Explain the differences in how and why Americans were treated. Analyze the effect of the different policies.

8. Compare the 1990s with one or more other time periods mentioned in the chronology of events that involve censorship issues. Predict how the decade will be assessed in terms of its approach to the issue.

9. Censorship of the Internet is the most current issue to be brought before the Supreme Court. Study the Chronology of Landmark Censorship Cases and research ones you think will set the precedents for the Internet issues.

10. *The Adventures of Huckleberry Finn* has been at the center of the censorship debate a number of times since its publication. Research the reasons for the concern. Analyze why those concerns became an issue in terms of the social context of the various time periods the debates occurred.

11. The Supreme Court might want to refer to the 1973 *Miller v. California* case to determine if Title V of the Communications Decency Act of 1996 is constitutional. Assume you are a law clerk for one of the justices. Prepare a brief that summarizes the case and explains if and how it is applicable to the issue at hand.

12. Assume you are a reporter attending the Supreme Court case involving censorship of the Internet. Write an article that would explain the issues of the case and the arguments for both sides in language that the general public would understand.

13. Research *Reno v. ACLU* (the case about the Internet) and make a list of the main points each side is trying to make. Research both the conservative and liberal stances on this issue and others involving censorship.

14. Write an editorial as it might appear in a newspaper that supports the conservative viewpoint on censorship. Also write an editorial from the perspective of a liberal newspaper.

15. Research the coverage of the Internet issue by the local and national media. Analyze the coverage with its political perspective.

16. One of the methods of communication on the Internet is e-mail. Research censorship issues concerning the postal service and relate them to e-mail.

17. The physical ability to limit access to the Internet might be extremely difficult to achieve. Use this information as the focal point of an argument for censoring the Internet.

18. Compare the Communications Decency Act to the voluntary rating systems for movies and television. Write a position paper on using rating systems to regulate speech.

19. Compare the Internet with forms of commercial communication such as movies and television. How do these forms of communication compare with literature?

21. How does needing technical knowledge to access the Internet impact on the argument for censorship? How does this information impact the issue of censorship and novels such as *The Catcher in the Rye?*

SUGGESTED READINGS

The following materials are useful research tools providing an overview of who bans books and why.

Blanshard, Paul. *The Right to Read—The Battle against Censorship*. Boston: Beacon Press, 1955.

Burress, Lee. *Battle of the Books*. Metuchen, N.J.: Scarecrow Press, 1989.

Burress, Lee, and Edward Jenkinson. *The Student's Right to Know*. Urbana, Ill.: National Council of Teachers of English, 1982.

Corbett, Edward J. "Raise High the Barriers, Censors." *America* (1961): 104. (Reprinted in *The National Catholic Weekly Review*. Boston: D.C. Heath and Co., 1963, 441–44.)

Costello, Donald P. "The Language of *The Catcher in the Rye.*" *American Speech* 34 (October 1959): 172–81.

Foerstel, Herbert N. *Banned in the U.S.A.: A Reference Guide to Book Censorship in School and Public Libraries*. Westport, Conn.: Greenwood Press, 1994.

Geller, Evelyn. *Forbidden Books in American Public Libraries*. Westport, Conn.: Greenwood Press, 1985.

Haight, Anne Lyon. *Banned Books—387* B.C. *to 1978* A.D. 4th ed. New York: R. R. Bowker, 1978.

Hurwitz, Leon. *Historical Dictionary of Censorship*. Westport, Conn.: Greenwood Press, 1985.

Jenkinson, Edward B. *Censors in the Classroom: The Mind Benders*. Carbondale: Southern Illinois University Press, 1979.

Jenkinson, Edward B. "Protecting Holden Caulfield and His Friends from the Censors." In Daniel Sheridan, ed., *Teaching Secondary English: Readings and Applications*, 331–45. New York: Longman, 1993.

Jorstad, E. "What Johnny Can't Read." *Commonweal* (17 June 1988).

Knoll, Erwin. "Bookburners." *The Progressive* (December 1985).

Lanier, Gene D. "Intellectual Freedom—That Neglected Topic. An Introduction." *North Carolina Libraries Magazine* (fall 1987).

Noble, William. *Bookbanning in America*. Middlebury, Vt.: Paul S. Eriksson, 1990.

"Special Report on Censorship" (Symposium). *Publishers Weekly* (11 July 1986).

West, M. I. "What Is Fit for Children?" *The New York Times Book Review*, 24 August 1986.

3

America's Postwar Culture

Culture is a slippery term meant to cast a wide umbrella over activities that, taken together, serve to define a civilization: myth and ritual, story and song, literature and art. Indeed, it is difficult to say with certainty what expressions should *not* be counted as one seeks to define the essence of a particular time and place. All this is made more vexing when considering a novel such as *The Catcher in the Rye*, because so much of Holden's world is circumscribed by his prep school milieu and his late adolescent sensibility. Nonetheless, Holden intuits, without realizing this consciously, that a much larger cultural world is throbbing away just beyond Pencey's gates; indeed, Holden experiences central aspects of post–War II culture during his "madman weekend" in Manhattan: his adventures in Greenwich Village, Central Park, the Edmont Hotel, or even his various cab rides.

Consider, for example, the following list of events that occurred in the years between the end of World War II in 1945 and the publication of *The Catcher in the Rye* in 1951:

1946   Robert Penn Warren publishes *All the King's Men*, arguably the best novel about politics written in America; Marc Chagall, Fernand Léger, and Saul Steinberg produce distinctively modernist works of art; and songs such as "Zip-a-dee-doo-dah" and "Shoo-fly Pie and Apple Pan Dowdy" top the popular music charts; Salinger publishes "Slight Rebellion Off Madison," his second story to include the misadventures of Holden Caulfield (the first appeared during the previous year), and a ninety-page novella about Holden is accepted but later withdrawn by Salinger.

1947   *The Diary of Anne Frank*, a work destined to become a classic of Holocaust literature, is published; Mickey Spillane's racy, hard-boiled detective novel, *I, the Jury*, becomes a best-seller that helps to change the attitude and interests of readers; Thor Heyrdahl sails on a raft from Peru to Polynesia in 101 days to prove prehistoric immigration; "flying saucers" are reported.

1948   Israel, the Jewish state, comes into existence; poet W. H. Auden publishes *The Age of Anxiety*, a work that gives a name to an increasingly unsettled time; T. S. Eliot wins the Nobel Prize in literature; 135 million paperback books—a phenomenon begun during World War II so that soldiers could have "pocket editions"—are sold; Alfred C. Kinsey publishes *Sexual Behavior in the Human Male*, his controversial study of sexual mores; Laurence Olivier wins the Academy Award for his psychologically-based performance of *Hamlet*.

1949   Arthur Miller's *Death of a Salesman*, a dazzling exploration of American dreams and interior nightmares, opens on Broadway (many will later regard it as the quintessential American play); William Faulkner, chronicler of the post–Civil War South, wins the Nobel Prize in literature; motion pictures of note include Carol Reed's *The Third Man* (with Orson Welles) and the film adaptation of Robert Penn Warren's *All the King's Men*; and "Rudolph, the Red-Nosed Reindeer" tops the pop-music charts on its way to becoming a holiday classic.

1950   Alger Hiss, a former U.S. State Department official, is sentenced for perjury in a case that continues to generate controversy and that first brought wide attention to prosecutor Richard Nixon; William J. Levitt, the suburban developer, is pictured on the cover of *Time* magazine (the suburban housing boom is going full swing with 1.4 million new houses started in 1950 alone); Ernest Hemingway, arguably the most "famous" serious writer in America, publishes *Across the River and into the Trees*, a novel critics roundly lambast; sociologist David Riesman publishes *The Lonely Crowd*, antihistamines become a popular remedy for colds and allergies; best-selling books include Henry Morton Robinson's *The Cardinal* and *Betty Crocker's Picture Cook Book*; the population of New York City hits the 7.8 million mark.

1951   North Korean forces break through at the 38th parallel and take Seoul; color television sets are introduced; Marlon Brando wows audiences with his performance of Stanley Kowolski in the film version of Tennessee Williams's *A Streetcar Named Desire*; J. D. Salinger publishes *The Catcher in the Rye*.

These are only highlights of the times and places that precede Holden's fictional appearance; taken together, they form the wider context that not only surrounds Holden as a character but also informs the readers of Salinger's novel. What cultural markers typified the years immediately following the end of World War II? More important, how does a general understanding of a novel's cultural context help us to better appreciate the references contained therein and those (consciously?) omitted? We begin with the following assertion by Frederick R. Karl, author of *American Fictions, 1940–1980*: "So much of major fiction in the 1950s is internalized, and therefore at odds with an extroverted country, because intensity of experience had already become the sole way one could remain valid, authentic, self-defined. Experience becomes in itself a goal, not something that can lead to some tangible success." Jeffrey Hart's *When the Going Was Good*, a conservative defense of the 1950s, disagrees with many of these assumptions, but in the conflict between the inherent value of rebelliousness and the claims on behalf of stability, one can begin to see something of how postwar culture developed. For Karl, the books that mattered most—that is, in terms of giving the 1950s its distinctive cultural thumbprint—were Paul Goodman's *Growing Up Absurd*, a plea for achieving an existentialist reality that neither accepts the system nor defiantly drops out; Jack Kerouac's *On the Road*, the quintessential novel of odyssey and beatnik adventure; and Norman Mailer's *The Naked and the Dead*, at once a war novel and a rumination on the nature of American politics. Karl, we should point out, did not think much of *The Catcher in the Rye* as a "serious" (rather than commercial) novel or as a penetrating study of its culture. Others felt quite differently; and as we look back at the 1950s from a nearly fifty-year retrospective, Salinger's novel is the one that most touches on the innocence and angst that wrestled throughout the postwar years until Vietnam drew a curtain on the suburban tract homes and conformist values that gave rise to such early television shows as *Leave It to Beaver* or *The Ozzie and Harriet Show*.

The years that followed the end of World War II are often spoken of as the Cold War, a period when culture and politics were often tragically intertwined. This was especially true as the House Un-American Activities Committee (HUAC) held hearings to determine if members of the entertainment industry were, by their definition, "now, or ever had been, members of the Communist Party." Once again, *innocence* becomes the operative word, as those whose youthful idealism during the 1930s had led them to embrace versions of left liberalism now found themselves under relentless scrutiny from those who worried (as it turns out, often with good reason) about subversive activities conducted by those who took marching orders from Moscow.

Granted, Holden is hardly a character embroiled with politics, unless one considers the world of Pencey as essentially "political." Instead, he divides everything that darts across his field of vision as either on the side of purity or on the side of corruption—with any evidences of maturity, much less adulthood, as proof positive of the latter. Politics of the Cold War variety simply don't enter into his consciousness. For example, of the teachers Holden remembers (most of them *un*fondly), none had been the subject of an investigation into a radical-political past. The witch-hunts conducted by the House Un-American Activities Committee do not intrude onto Pencey's conformist/pastoral life. It is enough that they were "teachers" for Holden to give them the fish eye. But as dark clouds moved across the national horizon, one detects ominous foreshadowings in Holden's insistence that the world remain in a condition of romantic purity, even as that same world pushes us toward complexity.

Excerpts from Douglas T. Miller and Marion Nowak's *The Fifties: The Way We Really Were* are particularly intriguing, first because one chapter ("Growing Up") focuses on teenagers in the 1950s and includes a number of references to Holden Caulfield. Its value, however, is in widening the cultural orbit from a single character in a very singular novel to a more general discussion of what it was like to "grow up" in the years immediately following World War II. In that chapter applications to Salinger's novel are obvious; however, the relationship between the two books is not always as self-evident. "The Happy Home Corporation and Baby Factory," the other chapter excerpted, contains a perspective *Catcher* largely omits—namely, that of women—that should be considered because so much of the culture of the 1950s revolved around marriage. Holden is certainly aware of women, although what he is mostly aware of is his confusion about how one ought to act with regard to them. His spirited, but ultimately pathetic defense of Jane Gallagher's honor is a case in point. Holden imagines the loss of Jane's virginity is a foregone conclusion, although the novel itself is less certain about what happened, or did not happen, during her date with the smooth-talking Stradlater. Holden, in short, is rather equally divided between wanting to be a full adult (as the culture defines it) by drinking hard liquor, smoking cigarettes, and seducing young women and the more sober realization that he is a flop at most of his efforts to act older than he, in fact, is.

The section continues with a brief discussion of the view of marriage held by Peter Tarnopol in *My Life as a Man*, a novel by Philip Roth, one of contemporary American literature's most important writers. A concluding excerpt is provided by Martha C. Nussbaum, classicist, moral philosopher, and feminist, as she recalls the "great deal of female misery . . . in those days."

Probably no category counts for more in the psychological makeup of American males than the attraction, indeed, the *lure*, of the West. The frontier has always served the American imagination as an unbounded space beyond the borders of religious sanctions and social restraints. There, as the myth would have it, one can at last be "free." Holden, too, dreams or, more correctly, fantasizes about a life much simpler than the one he experienced at Pencey and that he sees looming ahead as his cultural inheritance. No American writer has given us a better, more succinct definition of the West and its psychic pull than Robert Penn Warren does in his novel *All the King's Men*. We include an excerpt that puts the West into what can only be called a poetic reverie.

Finally, we include excerpts from book-length studies of Greenwich Village, Central Park, and jazz because these figure prominently in the novel and because they establish a necessary background to the culture Holden actually experiences. Greenwich Village, a section of Manhattan known for its bohemian culture and the various arts that flourish in its neighborhoods, is where Holden ruminates about jazz pianist "Old Ernie." Samuel B. Chartres and Leonard Kunstadt's *Jazz: A History of the New York Scene* chronicles the history of jazz in the Big Apple; and its concluding chapter, "Toward the Future," focuses on the Greenwich Village scene that Holden describes and that continued to flourish throughout the 1950s. The intention is not to identify one specific model for "Old Ernie," but rather to reveal him as a composite of a several influential musicians who moved from the be-bop of the 1940s to the "straight-ahead" jazz identified with the 1950s. We conclude our thumbnail sketch of postwar culture with "Scenes from a Park, 1941–1980," an especially rewarding chapter from Roy Rosenzweig and Elizabeth Blackmar's *The Park and the People: A History of Central Park*. Central Park has a variety of associations for Holden—from his nostalgic memories of grade school class trips to the Museum of Natural History, to the carousel on which his sister Phoebe rides in the novel's concluding tableau. The park has always seemed to be the very essence of New York City life, although it has of late acquired an unfortunate reputation as a crime-ridden locale. The excerpt from Rosenzweig and Blackmar's history of Central Park reminds readers of *The Catcher in the Rye* that this wasn't always the case and helps to establish the cultural context in which Holden can think about life's larger, more existential questions.

PERSPECTIVES IN AND OF THE 1950s

The view that the 1950s was a tame, largely sterile decade persists, although growing up during those years was both richer and more complicated than many imagine. In the following excerpts the authors draw from such disparate sources as *Life* magazine, baby doctor–guru Benjamin Spock, and various scholarly studies of conformity to illustrate how selective memory (whether fueled by nostalgia, political temperament, or other factors) helps to shape one's image of a decade. Although Holden can be used as a touchstone, it must also be remembered that there were those around him who did not share his nonconformist vision. Notice also the impact of popular music and films, many of which came after 1951—and after Holden's creation—but which, oddly enough, served as markers to his 1950s nonetheless.

FROM DOUGLAS T. MILLER AND MARION NOWAK, "GROWING
UP," IN *THE FIFTIES: THE WAY WE REALLY WERE*
(New York: Doubleday, 1977)

We tend to remember fifties youth in superficial ways. We think of the musical tastes, the dress habits, the conformity and status anxiety, sexual repressions, and political apathy of the young. These provide much of the stuff of fifties nostalgia. We recall (and often smile at) these complicated artifacts. But we recall them with an odd mix of feelings: with the affection anyone feels for those lost days of youth, with fondness for that simpler time, perhaps even with amusement tinged by unexamined pain. We try (and usually succeed) at forgetting the difficulties of being young in those years. In the fifties, America, like many another culture, sought to mold the young after its adult dreams. But the terrible conflicts that characterized fifties culture themselves distorted the mold. America's divided messages were crucial in determining the ways kids accepted their world, how they came to assert themselves in it and, eventually, even the ways they chose to rebel.

Youth occupied a unique place in fifties America. Teens were perceived as different from other human beings and so were more set apart by a generation gap. The value of being young kept rising. At the same time, Americans were returning (after the disciplinarian interlude of the twenties and thirties) to their traditional permissive child-rearing practices. Many other factors also converged to create the fifties teenager. Unprecedented affluence was coupled to the growth of the luxury businesses. These businesses saw the need to identify (that is, create) a separate youth market. This proved mutually beneficial: Teens bought youth products for the status and the sense of identity they received, and businesses provided these luxury needs to make money.

Out of such concepts came Dr. Benjamin Spock's *Common Sense Book of Baby and Child Care*. First published in 1946, Spock's book attained almost instant popularity. This was not because it presented any new ideas, but rather because it was a successful pastiche of ideas rising into the public awareness. Spock miniaturized the culture's child-rearing ideas in his book, and so gave them a larger vogue. Spock, of course, never advocated the licentious permissiveness for which he has since been blamed. If he can be faulted for anything, it is the subtle totalitarianism of his ideas. As Philip Slater has pointed out, many "Spockian parents feel that it is their responsibility to make their child into the most all-around perfect adult possible. . . . The child has his entire being involved with parental aspirations. What the child is not permitted to do is to take his own personality for granted."[1] This "mission to create a near perfect being" was also one more instance of American product orientation.[2]

NOTES

1. Philip Slater, *The Pursuit of Loneliness* (Boston: Beacon Press, 1970), p. 56.

2. Benjamin Spock, *Pocket Book of Baby and Child Care* (New York: Hawthorn Books, 1955), a mid-fifties paperback edition of the *Common Sense* volume first published in 1946; Slater, *Pursuit*, pp. 57, 69. By 1957 Spock's book had gone through 59 printings. The book sold about a million copies a year, becoming the biggest seller next to the Bible in American history.

Although Holden dabbles briefly with the idea of what "married life" might be like, it is hardly a serious option. But domesticity was what those only a few years older yearned for, settled into, and sometimes regretted. The last item—regret at career opportunities unrealized or resentment at the role the culture insisted they play—was particularly true for many women. In an age that specialized in television programs featuring contented housewives and full-time mothers, women who did not accept the constraints that purportedly came with marital bliss must have seemed odd indeed. In any event, the less such women said about their reservations (much less their "regrets"), the better.

Holden, in short, is not the only person who suffered from pressures to conform; and because Salinger's novel is so fixated on his problems, his perspective, and his voice, we thought it useful to add some information about the domestic realm that Holden largely takes for granted. As you read Miller and Nowak's chapter on how and why it was that women were trained and expected to "serve," think about the ways this material might alter your view of the 1950s as Holden experienced them.

FROM DOUGLAS T. MILLER AND MARION NOWAK, "THE HAPPY HOME CORPORATION AND BABY FACTORY," IN *THE FIFTIES: THE WAY WE REALLY WERE*
(New York: Doubleday, 1977)

Everybody got married in the fifties, or at least it was a supreme sign of personal health and well-being to be engaged in the social act of marriage and family-raising. "Whether you are a man or a woman," advised a widely read book called *The Woman's Guide to Better Living*, "the family is the unit to which you most genuinely belong. . . . The family is the center of your living. If it isn't, you've gone far astray." Men and women were marrying younger than ever. In 1950, census takers discovered, men's average marriage age was 22.0 and women's 20.3, a significant drop from 1940 figures of 24.3 and 21.5 respectively. More people were marrying. In 1955, family-living author Paul Landis estimated, 92 per cent of all Americans were or had been married, the highest record in national history. "Marriage is the *natural state* in adults," emphasized Landis.[1] In 1955, popular culture was saturated at all levels with this belief in the supreme wonderfulness of being married. It seemed so sane, healthy, *natural* for people to do that it became an absolute, unbending tenet of life.

NOTE

1. Dr. John A. Schindler, *A Woman's Guide to Better Living* (Garden City, N.Y., 1958), p. 415; Ben J. Wattenberg, *This U.S.A.* (Garden City, N.Y., 1965), p. 37.

Novelist Philip Roth expresses similar views about the pressures to marry in the 1950s in his 1974 novel *My Life as a Man*. In his case, however, the fictional marriage he chronicles is an unmitigated disaster that clearly has deep biographical roots and that he mulled over in a series of novels. Nonetheless, the sentiments of Roth's protagonist, Peter Tarnopol, are worth including here be-

cause they shine a vivid spotlight on the cultural patterns that surrounded Holden as he dreams of marrying a deaf-mute and living
a life far removed from the tensions and various pressures of growing up in the Manhattan of adult responsibility: "For those young
men who reached their maturity in the fifties, and who aspired to
be grown-up during that decade, when as one participant has written, everyone *wanted* to be thirty, there was considerable moral
prestige in taking a wife" (Roth, *My Life as a Man*, 169). Marriage
was a visible symbol of one's decency and, even more, of one's
maturity. Granted, just as Holden's bungled marriage proposal
shocks his date Sally Hayes, it also takes *our* breath away—because, despite his various protests, Holden hardly seems a candidate for being written down as "mature."

Indeed, as a struggling prep school student Holden is not in the
same condition as the considerably older Roth protagonist, but
Holden has an uncanny sense of the decade's cultural attitudes
nonetheless. He knows in his bones that marriage would change
his life enormously—even if he can't quite articulate the how or
why to Sally or even to himself. In *My Life as a Man*, Roth talks
about decency and maturity (a young man's "seriousness"), and
in certain respects Holden would probably agree, although he
would insist on adding the same litmus tests he brings to everything else—namely, is, or is not, marriage "phony"? His impulsive
(escapist?) proposal to Sally is a measure of just how confused and
how desperate he is at this point in the novel. As readers, we have
no reason to believe that this accident waiting to happen would
differ substantially from the troubled marriage of Holden's parents.
As to his fantasy wife and equally fantasized marriage, we are more
likely to smile and think of these passages as more examples of
the hypersensitive Holden who cannot quite bring himself to
throw a snowball because that would spoil the snow's essential
purity.

"No wonder," Roth points out, "that a young college-educated
bourgeois male of my generation who scoffed at the idea of marriage for himself, who would just as soon eat out of cans or in
cafeterias, sweep his own floor, make his own bed, and come and
go with no binding legal attachments, finding female friendship
and sexual adventure where and when he could, laid himself open
to the charge of 'immaturity' " (Roth, *My Life as a Man*, 169). Men
of the sort Roth describes marry so that they will not find them-

selves out of step in in the placid, conformist 1950s and also so that women might have some relief from the cultural restrictions that surround them like a wall.

Marriage, in short, struck Roth as the right thing to do, although much of this sentiment finds itself filtered through the tongue squarely in his cheek. Again, the marriage he goes on to describe is one in which an innocent male finds himself sacrificed on the marital altar. In some sense, Holden goes Roth one better, imagining as he does the benefits of a simple life lived in a pastoral, nonphony West. The right sort of wife—in Holden's case, a woman both deaf and mute—is just the ticket. One wonders why he neglects to mention checking out her teeth, because that, too, is of a piece with the other preconditions he imagines. Such a young man is a very young, young man. But, then again, there were those, male and female alike, who would have said much the same thing about Roth and his mouthpiece Peter Tarnopol. Maturity of the authentic sort cannot be willed into being, nor can it be achieved simply by entering into a legal arrangement with a woman. But for those who shared Roth's essential vision (and during the 1950s, this was many), the sheer challenge of marriage seemed attractive because it would forever divide males who remained little boys forever from those who gave themselves over to domesticity and the high probability of becoming fathers.

Many women, then and now, would strongly disagree with Roth's assessment about why men married in the 1950s. One of them, Martha Nussbaum (professor of classics and philosophy at the University of Chicago), remembers "growing up" during the 1950s and how less-than-subtle messages about sociocultural limitations were beamed to women during their high school and college years. Radicalized by the politics of the late 1960s, Nussbaum paints a picture of the general world Holden inhabited during his days at Pencey.

FROM MARTHA C. NUSSBAUM, "WOMEN IN THE SIXTIES," IN
REASSESSING THE SIXTIES: DEBATING THE POLITICAL AND
CULTURAL LEGACY
(Stephen Macedo, ed. New York: W. W. Norton, 1997)

In my high school class in 1964—a private girls' school in Bryn Mawr, Pennsylvania—there was just one working mother. Her work was understood by the gossip of the day to be a sign of economic distress. It was seen as a black mark against her husband since it was well understood that good men were good breadwinners whose wives did not need to leave the home. Because the family was weird in other ways as well (they had a lawn that looked like a jungle, and they were the only people I knew who drove a foreign car), they were socially rejected. It was no surprise when their daughter, my best friend, did not receive invitations to the formal predebutante dances known as the Junior Dance Assembly, to which I went with no pleasure at all. Nor was it any surprise when Sara ended up going to Oberlin College, a "pink" school, to which my father did not even permit me to apply. After all, they dressed very strangely, those Matheson women, wearing thick black stockings and shapeless tweeds and hair hung shapelessly straight down their backs, as they drove through Bryn Mawr laughing a little too loudly, in their bright yellow VW beetle.

There was a great deal of female misery in Bryn Mawr in those days, but it was on the whole unacknowledged silent misery. The immaculate lawns and elegant Georgian houses, three-inch heels, the carefully sprayed hairstyles, the long-sleek high-finned cars concealed from public view much depression and self-contempt, much aimless sadness, much diffuse and unfocused anger, much heavy idleness, much alcoholism— along with, and frequently subverting, much love and intelligence and hope. Sometimes, I am sure, this misery was conscious, and the women themselves could have said that they preferred and would choose another life. More often, aspirations having been blunted over the years, they could not have pictured to themselves a possible life that would be both theirs and more flourishing than the one they knew. They had been brought up to believe that fulfillment for a woman consisted in the sort of life they had, and so they felt that they should be happy. To the extent that a married woman was uncertain whether she was happy, she tended to sense that there was something wrong with her, for certainly the message of the times was there was nothing wrong with her world. She usually tried to conceal this unspecified flaw from others, frequently to some extent from herself. This limited her capacity to imagine other ways of life.

By contrast, Holden easily projects any number of imaginative alternatives to the socioeconomic realities his parents are planning for him. But he, too, is not oblivious to the pressures to someday marry—although Holden actively resists the tentacles of the insufferable Sally Hayes. No, what Holden wants—indeed, dreams about—is a wife who will be a deaf-mute (and, hence, as far from the babbling Sally Hayes as possible) but also—and importantly—that they will live out their days in a wholly imagined, wholly pastoral West. In this sense, Holden is in very good literary company, for the West of wide open spaces and individual freedom has always been seen as the alternative to crowded and conformist urban life. Thus, the West of the American imagination represents seemingly endless space, as well as boundless opportunity for those with gumption and a quick trigger finger. But as more probing fiction writers also understood, the West is where young men traditionally go when everything that had anchored their existence turns sour and the formerly solid melts into disarray.

Perhaps no American writer gets so quickly, or so lyrically, to the heart of these matters than Robert Penn Warren. His 1948 novel, *All the King's Men*, is the story of protagonist Jack Burden's initiation into the complexity and ruthlessness of American politics. A former Ph.D. candidate in history, Burden finds himself working as a research assistant/operative for Willie Stark, a corrupted politician modeled on Louisiana's populist governor Huey Long. As the nets around Burden tighten, and he begins to see his own complicity in evil, he suddenly pulls up stakes and heads west: "For West is where we all plan to go someday. It is where you go when the land gives out and the old-field pines encroach. It is where you go when you get the letter saying: Flee, all is discovered. It is where you go when you look down at the blade in your hand and see the blood on it. It is where you go when you are told that you are a bubble on the tide of empire" (Warren, *All the King's Men*, 270). Granted, Burden (yes, his name is significant) does not yet know about the burdens of history, nor can he fit the pieces of his shattered life into a coherent portrait. In this sense, he resembles Oedipus Rex, the man who is out to discover the murderer of the king, only to learn painfully that the murderer is himself.

By contrast, Holden is hardly a Jack Burden, much less an Oedipus Rex. But he does duplicate the essential pattern of American escapism (usually male) and the American West. Once again, parallels between Holden and Huck Finn announce themselves because just as Huck does not realize just how lawless and ugly the Indian territories he's lighting out for at the end of the novel are, Holden is likely to find a West without subways, high-rise apartments, or the other amenities of urban culture. In short, both protagonists are destined to be disappointed, despite the briefs each files against what Huck calls "sivilization" and Holden deems as phoniness.

NEW YORK CITY JAZZ

Jazz is nearly as much about ambience and performance as it is about music. In *The Catcher in the Rye*, jazz artist Old Ernie is a study in the ways that fame can lead to corruption—at least so far as Holden is concerned. But, then again, Holden means to distance himself from the overly adoring fans who crowd into a Greenwich Village nightspot to see Ernie do his legendary stuff. What stands at the center of this portion of the novel, however, is the impact of jazz on an increasing segment of the hip and wanna-be hip. As Holden's descriptions make clear, jazz clubs were a favorite haunt of "Joe College" types—no doubt because they associated the clubs with sophistication. In this sense, Ernie is meant to suggest jazz in its commercial (mainstream?) guise, rather than the more experimental, "cooler" sounds coming from small clubs that most college kids wouldn't know about.

Despite Holden's sense of himself as a jazz buff, he makes his way down to the Village because jazz clubs were one of the few places where the underaged could be served alcoholic drinks without a hassle. For the Holden who wants to be counted as an adult (ironically enough, at the same time he insists on preserving the uncorrupted innocence he associated with childhood), hanging around in Greenwich Village jazz spots makes a (self-conscious) statement. In this sense, Holden is probably no hipper than the college crowd he makes fun of, although the way he will later describe a soulful phonograph recording he buys for Phoebe (and subsequently breaks into pieces) suggests that he knows the difference between authentic sounds and faked ones. The same thing is true about his observations about Old Ernie hamming it up for the crowd. If his talent still remains, it has gotten tangled up in applause that now comes too easily and no longer has to be earned.

By contrast, Samuel B. Chartres and Leonard Kunstadt's *Jazz: A History of the New York Scene* chronicles the rise of jazz in New York City from music halls like Tony Pastor's or Weber and Fields's in the 1890s to the present. The story of jazz in cities such as New Orleans, Kansas City, or Chicago is well known; but, in truth, the New York jazz connection may well be the most colorful and important of them all. The excerpt that follows provides some of the flavor that attracted Holden to jazz clubs as well as specific information about jazz artists that might inspire further study. This is the Real Deal—and it was happening at the very moment when Holden was giving the novel's one jazz musician the fish eye.

FROM SAMUEL B. CHARTRES AND LEONARD KUNSTADT, *JAZZ: A HISTORY OF THE NEW YORK SCENE*
(New York: Da Capo Press, 1981)

By the late 1950s jazz had become one of the biggest entertainment industries in the United States. Jazz records, most of them produced by the companies in New York, sold in the hundreds of thousands. Jazz festivals had become a colorful part of the American holiday season. The city itself was the scene of hundreds of jazz concerts, from the uninhibited Dixieland concerts held in the early morning hours in Carnegie Hall to the esoteric experimentation of the concerts in small theaters and halls in Greenwich Village.

. . . Mainstream jazz referred to the jazz of the swing era and "mainstream" musicians such as Harry Edison and Buck Clayton found themselves in demand for a number of small, informal recording sessions that often resulted in pleasantly swinging, if somewhat lackluster jazz. The most positive result of the new interest in "mainstream" was a return to popularity of both Duke Ellington and Count Basie, who had found themselves pushed aside by the excitement over the newer jazz styles. There was even a festival appearance by a re-creation of the old Fletcher Henderson Orchestra, which included men like (Coleman) Hawkins who had worked with Henderson for many years. Jazz has achieved such great popularity that there has been room for the "cool" musicians, for the "funky" school, for the "mainstream" musicians, and even for a number of men, such as the tenor-saxophone player John Coltrane, who played a fervid modern style usually called "hard hop." Among the leading "hard hoppers" was another tenor-saxophone player named Sonny Rollins who showed considerable promise as a creative soloist in the fifties, but who has not played regularly in public for some time. One of the most popular of the New York "hard hop" groups has been the Jazz Messengers, a quintet led by the colorful and talented drummer Art Blakey, who played an important part in the recordings made by Thelonious Monk in the late forties and early fifties. . . .

A number of trio records with the drummer Art Blakey and several different bass players, made in the late forties and early fifties first for Blue Note Records and then Prestige Records, began to attract for Monk an audience outside of the small circle of musicians who knew his music. Blakey's work on drums was particularly successful, and he seemed to he able to anticipate the subtleties of Monk's phrasing. Often Monk has been criticized for a lack of melody, but solos such as "Ruby, My Dear" on Blue Note 549 are evidence of a melodic sense that is able to express sensitive emotion. Other trio recordings, such as "Little Rootie Tootie" on Prestige 850, are unnerving on first encounter, but the immense gusto and highly developed ironic sense in much of Monk's music of this period give his performances a continuing freshness and spontaneity. Probably his most remarkable recordings were a series of band recordings made for Blue Note between 1947 and 1952. He scored a number of his own compositions for five- and six-piece groups and was able to impress his own ideas on the other musicians to such an extent that these band performances remain classics of their kind. Some of his best-known compositions—" 'Round about Midnight," "Misterioso," "Off Minor," "Criss-Cross," "Epistrophy," "Well, You Needn't," "In Walked Bud"—were recorded during this time. There was even an astonishing recording of the old waltz "Carolina Moon," with the bass playing in 6/8 tempo against the 3/4 of the horns. Often Monk plays rather sketchily behind a soloist, but for "Carolina Moon" his backings were painstaking in their clarity.

Monk worked only occasionally around New York. He took the first bop group into Greenwich Village when he opened at the Village Vanguard on Seventh Avenue in 1948, but his public appearances were not generally successful. His personality was as individual as his music, and audiences often found him difficult to watch. His first major success occurred in 1957, when he took a quartet into a small club called the Five Spot on the upper edges of the Bowery. John Coltrane was playing tenor; Wilbur Ware, bass; and Shadow Wilson, drums. The Five Spot is not a large place, with the piano only a few feet from the bar, and Monk's presence seemed to fill the room.

CENTRAL PARK

New York City's Central Park figures prominently in the plot of *The Catcher in the Rye*, not only as the place where Holden has fond memories of trips to the Museum of Natural History but also where he has his final, revelatory moment with Phoebe. For New Yorkers Central Park suggests a great many things: a dividing line between the city's East and West Side; the swank Tavern on the Green restaurant; bike paths, ball fields, and jogging paths; and, perhaps most of all, a place of respite from concrete streets and urban tension. For Holden, it is the pastoral incarnate, a place removed from the getting-and-spending that characterizes the swank shops and four-star hotels of Manhattan's Fifth Avenue. Although it should be noted that Holden takes the public space largely for granted, however much he seems obsessed about the fate of its ducks during icy winters. To provide a fuller sense of the park's history, especially at a time when it was *not* associated with personal danger and crime, we have included excerpts from Roy Rosenzweig and Elizabeth Blackmar's *The Park and the People: A History of Central Park*.

FROM ROY ROSENZWEIG AND ELIZABETH BLACKMAR, "SCENES FROM A PARK, 1941–1980," IN *THE PARK AND THE PEOPLE: A HISTORY OF CENTRAL PARK* (Ithaca, N.Y.: Cornell University Press, 1992)

In the early spring of 1950 an errant-baseball narrowly missed the head of Iphigene Ochs Sulzberger. The ball had come from the Great Lawn of Central Park, the site she and other preservationists had fought so hard to turn into a pastoral meadow. Walking across the park, she was "shocked" to discover that the parks department had just installed several permanent baseball backstops on the Great Lawn. "I suppose it is too late to do anything about this," she wrote in a letter of complaint to her friend Bob Moses, then in his seventeenth year as park commissioner (just as she was in her seventeenth year as president of the Park Association of New York City). She proposed, nonetheless, that a fence might prevent injuries to passersby. She also advised Moses to see that the playground in the northwest corner of the Great Lawn was paved—"it is now nothing but a sea of mud under the children's play apparatus."[1]

Visitors to the Great Lawn in 1950 could see the full fabric of Moses' vision of Central Park as a place of baseball backstops, asphalt, and efficiency. If they had returned again three decades later, they could have glimpsed the unraveling of Moses' vision. On June 12, 1982, three-quarters of a million people packed themselves onto the Great Lawn to denounce the nuclear arms race and to urge a freeze on the production of nuclear weapons. Some said it was the largest single protest demonstration in American history. Moses, who had been dead scarcely a year, would have detested both the demonstrators' politics and their use of Central Park for any political purpose.

1. Iphigene Sulzberger to Robert Moses, Mar. 27, 1950. B 102850, Pks. Dpt., MARC.

New York City is rightly regarded as America's capital of culture. Holden is hardly a candidate to work for its public relations department, but his journey/quest through the streets of Manhattan makes the most of the appropriate cultural stops nonetheless. From Holden we get a sense of the city's museums, its Broadway theater district, its movie theaters, its jazz clubs, and the magnificence of Central Park. Even more important, what Holden's impressions of culture come to are the alternating rhythms of attraction and repulsion that lie at the very heart of Holden's character. In this sense, the street skates that city kids wear (and the straps that fasten them to their shoes) are as much a cultural artifact as are the unchanging exhibits in the Museum of Natural History or the fact that Sally Hayes is hardly the only person in the Broadway house who "adores" the Lunts.

Is what we've been describing more evidence that Holden is a child of privilege? Possibly, but culture often makes its impact in subtle ways that even Holden's arch attitude cannot entirely dismiss. Why so? Because culture is ubiquitous, and because it gives us the image and the postures by which we conduct our public lives and that often give shape to our private dreams. Protest though he might, Holden is—in this single sense—very much "one of us," regardless of our economic class or where we might happen to live.

STUDY QUESTIONS

1. The culture of postwar America is evident throughout *The Catcher in the Rye*. Identify those aspects of the culture during the present time period that are evident in the novel.

2. Consider how the novel would be affected in terms of its cultural aspects if it had been written fifty years *earlier*.

3. Describe how the culture of the 1950s influences Holden's behavior in general.

4. How do the values of the postwar period impact on Holden's attitudes and behavior toward women? Point out specific scenes from the novel to support your points.

5. Explain how the women depicted in *The Catcher in the Rye* reflect or contradict the role of women in the late 1940s and early 1950s.

6. Holden considers himself a rebel to the cultural values of his time. Assess his self-evaluation in terms of his actions and words.

7. The late 1940s and 1950s are often called the "age of conformity." Find specific scenes from *The Catcher in the Rye* that support or disprove that theory.

8. The Cold War had affected many aspects of the culture by the time *The Catcher in the Rye* was published. Yet there aren't any specific references to it. Give your opinion why Salinger chose not to include this cultural aspect in his novel. Explain why or why not you would include such information if you were writing a novel about teenagers during that time.

9. Reflect on the time period of your own high school days. What, if any, historic references might you use if you were writing a novel about teenagers today?

10. A survey in "Growing Up" mentions that a number of teenagers in the 1950s felt their teachers had radical ideas. Explain why or why not Holden would agree with the statement. How do you think Holden would feel if he did have teachers with radical ideas? Why?

11. The excerpt from "Growing Up" describes parents of the 1950s as being permissive. Explain how the authors would rate Holden's parents. Support you opinion with examples from the novel.

12. Dr. Spock, the noted baby doctor, is mentioned in "Growing Up." How would he rate Holden's parents?

13. Compare teenagers today with those of Holden's generation. Would you label either group naive or cynical? Why?

TOPICS FOR WRITTEN OR ORAL EXPLORATION

1. Some of the highlights of American culture in terms of music, art, and literature are included in the chronology at the beginning of this chapter. Most would be considered classics; that is, they have found a place in history. Prepare a chronology that includes works and events from each of the last ten years that you think will become highlights or classics.

2. Make a list of the historical events and important people who would be included in your chronology.

3. If you were preparing to write a novel that would reflect the most important cultural aspects of the present time, what would they be?

4. To many, the 1950s invokes a picture of life in the tract homes of suburban America. In what ways does the information included in the excerpts about New York City depict a culture similar to, or different from, that picture?

5. Compare and contrast how "The Happy Home Corporation" and "Growing Up" depict life in the 1950s.

6. The article "Growing Up" begins: " 'The teenagers of today,' remarked a mid-fifties commentator, 'are stronger, smarter, more self-sufficient and more constructive than any other generation in history.' " Justify the commentator's statements.

7. Compare and contrast the teenagers of the 1950s as depicted in "Growing Up" with teenagers today.

8. Prepare an argument that defends the teenagers from the criticisms made about them in "Growing Up."

9. Describe the criticisms you would include if you were writing a chapter about teenagers today.

10. Describe the good qualities you would include if you were writing a chapter about teenagers today.

11. "Growing Up" cites a study done in the 1950s that states that 59 percent of teenagers felt that "a lot of teachers, these days, have radical ideas that have to be watched." Explain the impact of that statement within the context of the cultural/historical period.

12. If you were preparing a survey for teenagers today, explain why you would or would not include a question about the radical ideas of teachers.

13. List the kinds of ideas that the students might have thought were radical for teachers to have in the 1950s. List the ideas students would think are radical for teachers to have today. Research what happened

to teachers with those ideas in the 1950s. Compare that to what happens to teachers in the same position today.

14. Prepare a defense for a teacher you would have supported in the 1950s. Compare it to a defense you might prepare for a teacher today. If your defenses are different, explain why.

15. The youth of the 1950s were dubbed the "Silent Generation." Prepare an oral report assessing the validity of the characterization.

16. The "Silent Generation" is used to characterize teenagers of the 1950s. Develop terms to characterize the youth for each decade since the 1950s. Explain reasons you chose each term.

17. Research current child-raising approaches. Compare them with the ones attributed to Dr. Spock. How do Dr. Spock's ideas fit in today's society?

18. The excerpt from "Growing Up" refers to the importance of teenagers to the economy. Research if this statement is still true. Prepare a visual presentation showing which products cater to teenagers by their advertising campaigns.

19. Music and films are important characteristics of culture. They often reflect the attitudes of the people and the times. In terms of teenagers, they often promote a point of view. Study the music or films of each of the decades from the postwar period to the present. Present excerpts which agree or disagree with the statement, Music and film often promote teenage rebelliousness and articulate teenage anxieties.

SUGGESTED READINGS

The following books focus on aspects of the culture of the 1950s on either a general or a specific level. They were chosen not only to supplement the information included in this sourcebook but also to provide students and teachers with directions for future research.

Agar, Herbert. *The Price of Power: America since 1945*. Chicago: University of Chicago Press, 1957.

Allen, Frederick Lewis. *The Big Change: America Transforms Itself 1900–1950*. New York: Harper, 1952.

Bell, Daniel. *The End of Ideology: On the Exhaustion of Political Ideas in the Fifties*. Revised ed. New York: Free Press, 1965.

Brooks, John. *The Great Leap: The Past Twenty-Five Years in America*. New York: Harper & Row, 1966.

Buckley, William F., Jr. *God and Man at Yale: The Superstitions of Academic Freedom*. Chicago: H. Regnery Co., 1957.

Cook, Bruce. *The Beat Generation*. New York: Scribner, 1971.

Degler, Carl N. *Affluence and Anxiety, 1945–Present*. Glenview, Ill.: Scott, Foresman, 1968.

Goodman, Paul. *Growing Up Absurd*. New York: Ingram, 1960.

Hart, Jeffrey. *When the Going Was Good*. New York: Crown, 1982.

Karl, Frederick R. *American Fiction, 1940–1980: A Comprehensive History & Critical Evaluation*. New York: HarperCollins, 1985.

Karson, Albert, and Perry E. Gianakos, eds. *American Civilization since World War II: Readings on Its Character, Style, and Quality*. Belmont, Calif.: Wadsworth Publishing Co., 1968.

Kerouac, Jack. *On the Road*. New York: Penguin, 1957.

Mailer, Norman. *The Naked and the Dead*. New York: Rinehart, 1948.

Roth, Philip. *My Life as a Man*. New York: Holt, Rinehart and Winston, 1974.

Stone, I. F. *The Haunted Fifties*. New York: Random House, 1963.

Valentine, Alan C. *The Age of Conformity*. Chicago: H. Regnery Co., 1954.

Warren, Robert Penn. *All the King's Men*. New York: Harcourt Brace, 1948.

Zinn, Howard. *Postwar America: 1945–1971*. Indianapolis: Bobbs-Merrill, 1973.

Zornow, William Frank. *America at Mid-Century: The Truman Administration, the Eisenhower Administration*. Cleveland: H. Allen, 1959.

4

Preparatory Schools

Pencey Prep does not exist anymore than does Holden Caulfield himself. But Salinger's portrait of prep school life has more than a few correspondences to the genuine article. Most critics agree that Salinger drew from his own experiences at Valley Forge Military Academy, altering the names of the Peddie School and Peddington Prep until it became "Pencey," and added dashes of local color from such elitist prep schools as Phillips Andover, Choate, and Lawrenceville.

Addressing the National Education Association in 1873, James McCosh, president of Princeton University, argued that "the grand educational want of America . . . is a judiciously scattered body of secondary schools, to bring on our brighter youth from what has been so well commenced in the primary schools, and may be so well completed in the better colleges." What he called for, in short, was a network that would supply well-prepared college freshmen and thus raise the intellectual prestige of a college diploma. The preparatory schools he had in mind would fuse the best elements of English "public school" (the British term for what we, in the United States, call private schools)—principally, Eton and Harrow—with the best attributes of the American democratic spirit. In addition to rigorous academic preparation, prep schools emphasized athletics (as the British liked to boast, the Battle of Waterloo had been won on the playing fields of Eton), codes of the gentleman, and the values of noblesse oblige appropriate to those who would one day wield enormous power and influence. Others were more critical, preferring to think of prep schools as simply bastions of privilege and snobbery.

Whichever view one holds (Holden would side with the prep school knockers), the facts of the matter are that schools such as Groton (founded in 1884), Hotchkiss (founded in 1891), and the Middlesex School (founded in 1903) have flourished in the twentieth century and that the number of American high school students who attend such prestigious institutions remains only a tiny fraction of the whole. Moreover, preppies have been the object of satire long after Holden Caulfield held their mores up to ridicule. For example, Erich Segal's *Love Story* (1970) makes much of the fact that Oliver's lower-middle-class girlfriend gets his goat by calling him "Preppy," and when Ali McGraw played the role in the novel's film adaptation (to Ryan O'Neil's Oliver), the result made the class conflicts that prep school set into motion abundantly clear. Lisa Birnbach's *The Official Preppy Handbook* (1980) added whole new installments to the satire one could make about students who bedeck themselves in the latest fashions from the L. L. Bean catalog or who in other ways try to create the illusion that they have "prepped" for college rather than simply attended the normal classes of a normal public high school.

Among Holden's ruminations are those that center on the yawning gap between what schools such as Pencey officially stand for and what, in fact, they actually are; how money divides people (this, despite Holden's reckless abandon in terms of spending it and his own instances of snobbery); and the education he did, or did not receive, while "prepping." Indeed, the charged word here may well be *preparatory*, because Holden is caught in a world where the major focus is to "prepare" one for college work and life, while Holden is not at all sure that adulthood is a good thing, much less what he particularly wishes for himself.

To enhance your understanding and discussion of this topic, we have included a number of documents that should help to put the prep school milieu into perspective. These include an excerpt from Ian Hamilton's quasi-biographical study, *In Search of J. D. Salinger;* interviews with a wide range of prep school graduates; excerpts from the 1951 catalog of the Peddie School; and an excerpt from

Peter W. Cookson, Jr. and Caroline Hodges Persell's *Preparing for Power: America's Elite Boarding Schools.*

As you read through this material, try to balance your own high school experiences against those of Holden but also think about the way that class interests are factored (sometimes consciously, sometimes not) into the formula. Some elements that Holden rails against (materialism, general phoniness, and the special pains of being an outsider) will be common to any high school student, but others are particular to those living away from home and in the pressure-cooker environment that prep schools often create. Finally, think about how one might distinguish between environment and inclination—that is, between the extent that being in a prep school affects Holden's personality versus the sense that he would be a misfit, a rebel no matter where he happened to be.

SALINGER AS SUBJECT

Put charitably, Salinger is extraordinarily protective of his privacy. Not only does he live the life of a recluse, refusing all invitations to give public readings, grant interviews, or even answer letters, but he also insists that his friends join him in this self-imposed wall of silence. So, when Ian Hamilton, author of a widely respected biography of the poet Robert Lowell, chose Salinger as a subject, most people figured that he was in for trouble. Hamilton knew full well how uncooperative Salinger had been with other journalists who sought him out, but he hoped that his project would strike a sympathetic chord. In a retrospective essay entitled "The Biographer's Misgivings" (in *Walking Possession: Essays and Reviews, 1968–1993* [Reading, MA: Addison-Wesley, 1996]), Hamilton puts it this way: "Perhaps he was waiting for the really *serious* approach—from *the biographer*. Perhaps he was waiting for *me*." Salinger, however, wasn't; he not only fended off Hamilton's dogged efforts but also took him to court when the biographer quoted portions from Salinger's letters. The celebrated case established the writer's control over such material and made Hamilton substantially revise the book we know as *In Search of J. D. Salinger*.

Still, there are valuable things one can learn about Salinger even if Hamilton's book is not quite the biography he had hoped it would be. For example, Salinger's prep school experiences will be of considerable interest to students of *The Catcher in the Rye*, even if one must make generous allowances for the liberties that fiction takes with fact. As you read Hamilton's account, weigh the J. D. Salinger he chronicles against the Holden Caulfield whom Salinger created.

FROM IAN HAMILTON, *IN SEARCH OF J. D. SALINGER*
(New York: Random House, 1986)

Salinger has said that he hated life at military school, but the evidence is contradictory. . . . In fact, his career at Valley Forge is marked by a curiously companionable struggle between eager conformity and sardonic detachment. His co-students tend to remember the sardonic side:

What I remember most about Jerome was the way he used to speak. He always talked in a pretentious manner as if he were reciting something from Shakespeare. And he had a sort of sardonic wit.

I must say I enjoyed his company immensely. He was full of wit and humor and sizzling wisecracks. He was a precocious and gifted individual, and I think he realized at that age that he was more gifted with the pen than the rest of us.

We were both skinny adolescents and must have looked terribly young and boyish. I was immediately attracted to him because of his sophistication and humor. His conversation was frequently laced with sarcasm about others and the silly routines we had to obey and follow at school. . . . Both of us hated the military regime and often wondered why we didn't leave the school. He enjoyed breaking the rules, and several times we both slipped off the academy grounds at 4 A.M. to enjoy a breakfast in the local diner. It was a great surprise to me that he returned to school for a second year.

He loved conversation. He was given to mimicry. He liked people, but he couldn't stand stuffed shirts. Jerry was aware that he was miscast in the military role. He was all legs and angles, very slender, with a shock of black hair combed backward. . . . He always stuck out like a sore thumb in a long line of cadets.

Hamilton does not name his interviewees because they insisted on anonymity (such is the continuing mystique in which those who knew Salinger have sworn themselves to secrecy or at least discretion), but one can get a sense of the young Salinger's complex, often contradictory character from what his classmates at Valley Forge Military Academy had to say about him.

INTERVIEWS WITH PREP SCHOOL SURVIVORS

No doubt there are autobiographical elements in Salinger's portrait of Holden Caulfield, but rather than pursue the connections (as Hamilton's study tries to do), it is wiser to think of Holden as a composite portrait. This view is strengthened by the selections of interviews with prep school graduates drawn from a wide range of experiences and impressions.

Wes Kaplan is a native New Yorker whose schooling reflects educational realities—and life—for upscale Manhattanites during the 1980s and 1990s. He spent his primary grades at Alan Stevenson, widely known as a "feeder school" (that is, a school with a long history of supplying students to elite colleges), in his case, the preparation led him to the Browning School, located on Manhattan's Upper East Side. Kaplan graduated in 1997. He is currently enrolled at Franklin and Marshall College. While the following impressions are clearly his own, there are good reasons to believe that Kaplan speaks for many very recent graduates of prep schools.

INTERVIEW WITH WES KAPLAN (1998)

Pinsker: Let me start with the obvious question: Have you read *The Catcher in the Rye*?

Kaplan: Yes, I have . . . a long time ago.

Pinsker: How long ago? Surely not when you were three or when you were four. So, when?

Kaplan: Seventh grade. [Kaplan was thirteen years old.]

Pinsker: As I understand it, Browning is not a residential school. Located in the city, students return to their homes after classes and extracurricular activities are over. Given that fact, what do you figure are the differences between your prep school experience and Holden's?

Kaplan: Once you leave home for school, things change dramatically. You're on your own and you carry more responsibilities—not only in terms of your academic work but social interactions as well. In fact, you're now responsible for *everything*. It's easier to attend a day school rather than a residential preparatory—easier in terms of academic work and easier in terms of living arrangements.

Pinsker: When you think of Holden and his complaint that Pencey students are cliquish and phony, do these accusations strike you as also true about the Browning School?

Kaplan: Not really, although there were many other prep schools I visited that were top-heavy with cliques as well as with Holden wanna-bes. You know, the leader-of-the-pack syndrome.

Pinsker: But Holden, either in his eyes or ours, hardly qualifies as a leader of the pack. If anything, he is the person who consciously chooses to stand *outside* the pack.

Kaplan: True, but he felt that everyone was a phony except himself.

Pinsker: He was *better* than the pack—right? And would this be especially true at some of the prep schools you visited?

Kaplan: Yes. Take Andover, for example. When I spent some time there with a boyhood friend, you couldn't help but notice the cliques. Everybody hangs out with a certain crowd, and very few people even talk to people outside their particular circle. Holden would probably take the whole bunch to task as "phonies."

Pinsker: Holden, as you know, is very critical of people who make, or want to make, money—this, despite (or perhaps because) he comes from money himself. Ambition, materialism, even the work ethic itself seem to Holden to be bad things. Do you recall any of your classmates who expressed the same feelings?

Kaplan: Actually, a lot of my classmates at Browning felt pretty much as Holden does. Maybe as many as half. The first group is exactly as Holden describes the average Pencey student: aware that they have money and that they are very privileged. Often they are— or become—snobbish. And then there are others who come from money, and they don't think of it as a big deal. It just *is*.

Pinsker: Are there those who are hypercritical of fellow students with money?

Kaplan: Not that I particularly noticed.

Pinsker: Did you know any students at Browning who deeply identified with Holden?

Kaplan: One, and I would say that he only had a brush with Holden-like attitudes and behavior.

Pinsker: Well, put another way, did you know students who thought of Holden as one terrific jerk?

Kaplan: Absolutely . . . including me, at least until the end of the novel.

Pinsker: Is this because Holden doesn't want to fit, *won't* fit in—and he wants you to like him for precisely these reasons?

Kaplan: Exactly.

Pinsker: Did you have teachers at Browning that you found memorable—either memorably good or memorably bad?

Kaplan: Absolutely. What I noticed was a wide variety of teaching styles and teachers. I can't say that any were memorably "bad," and besides, that would only be a personal opinion. Some provided us with a syllabus for the course and allowed us to pretty much work at our own pace; others nursed you along every step of the way. But I can say this: my senior English teacher was, by far, my favorite. He struck just the right balance between allowing us freedom and giving us disciplined instruction when we needed it.

Pinsker: Suppose I argued that parents send their children to private schools in New York City for safety reasons; and this, more than anything else, accounts for the world you experienced in K–12.

Kaplan: I would probably agree.

Pinsker: But that wasn't Holden's situation. His parents sent him to Pencey to prepare him to do well in some prestigious college, and then to do the same in corporate or professional America. On the other hand, would it be fair to say that many Manhattan parents send their children to city prep schools so that they will come home at the end of the day "alive" rather than stabbed to death?

Kaplan: I suppose, although safety is probably the sole issue in grades K–9; after that, parents also look for a school that will get their child into one of the better, more competitive colleges.

Pinsker: When you read *The Catcher in the Rye*, is the certain experience of that novel very close, or very far, from your own experiences at Browning?

Kaplan: I guess what I still like about the book is that you can relate to it, even if some of the details of prep school life have changed.

Pinsker: Are you suggesting that what makes Holden's story so universal is that it is simultaneously a tale of confusion and an account of adolescent pain?

Kaplan: I guess so, although I would simply say that I find it easy to identify with many of the characters, even though none of them is me *exactly*.

Pinsker: Any final thoughts?

Kaplan: Well, I would just want to emphasize that the private school experience—with one's teachers or friends—tends to be more powerful. Because the numbers of a class size are much smaller than in public schools, you get to know everyone more intensely. There were twenty-two students in my graduating class at the Browning School, and it just felt like I knew every single person. Indeed, I did. And it was either "good powerful" or "bad powerful." By that I mean, relationships were either black or white—you liked somebody a lot or you couldn't stand him. There weren't people you just knew casually and could be indifferent about.

Pinsker: Do you think that this would have been even more the case had you attended a residential prep school?

Kaplan: I don't think it would have been more intense. The transition from living at home to living away at school is what determines intensity—and if that happens during high school or later on at college, it really doesn't matter. But being surrounded by powerful relationships helps to push this intensity in the right direction. It's only advantageous, whenever it comes.

Since 1980 Steven Bender has been teaching in the English Department of the Dalton School, located in New York City. Although not a product of the prep school system himself, he has had a wide experience working with adolescents in this environment. Like the Browning School, Dalton is not residential—although extracurricular activities often keep students on its campus until the early evening.

INTERVIEW WITH STEVEN BENDER (1998)

Pinsker: Do the students you typically see still tend to read *The Catcher in the Rye?*

Bender: At Dalton, all students read it in the eighth grade, as part of their required reading. So, yes, they know it by the time they get to me.

Pinsker: Do many of them continue to identify with Holden as the lonely outsider who doesn't fit in?

Bender: I don't know about "many," but I suppose that the answer is yes. Many students identify on some level with Holden and go out of their way to define themselves as "different." The range runs from the ridiculous (turned-around baseball caps, colored hair, various piercings), to the more authentic—kids with genuine artistic sensibilities (kids who write poetry for the literary magazine, who do senior projects in film) who do feel alienated from the culture of the school. Maybe they feel different because they really are.

Pinsker: Can what you're describing be called yet another instance of "lonely" and loving it?

Bender: I suppose, although this is probably more a reflection of adolescent confusion and posturing than of anything that can be pinned on a private school environment.

Pinsker: Why so?

Bender: Because *The Catcher in the Rye*, while it happens to be set on a prep school campus, is really about the pains of growing up in what Holden sees as a corrupt adult world. Sensitive teenagers— wherever they happen to be in high school—know this, and for many of them Holden is a hero.

Pinsker: What about the ones Holden calls "phonies"? Do they think he's so wonderful?

Bender: Probably not, but I'd just be guessing. A lot has changed since Holden fought his various battles at Pencey. For example, the pressure to get good grades and ultimately an admission letter from a good college is something that contemporary parents and children now share. For such people, Holden is likely to be written off as a "loser." It wasn't always this way.

Nate Gasdsen, a native of Harrisburg, Pennsylvania, is a forty-five-year-old African American who attended Phillips Exeter Academy during the years between 1967 and 1969. He was among the first significant group of African Americans to attend Phillips Exeter. The national consciousness-raising that accompanied the Civil Rights movement partly explains the scholarship he received along with the culture shock and ambivalence he has been struggling with ever since. After graduation, Gasdsen went in and out of various colleges, finally receiving his degree from Pennsylvania State University at Harrisburg. He has worked in radio and as a journalist. For the past four years he has been a member of the English Department of J. P. McCaskey High School in Lancaster, Pennsylvania. He is at work on a memoir about his experiences at Phillips Exeter Academy.

INTERVIEW WITH NATE GASDSEN (1998)

Pinsker: I take it that you've read *The Catcher in the Rye*.

Gasdsen: Yes, although it's been awhile.

Pinsker: Are there a lot of resonances as you compare Holden's experiences at Pencey with yours at Phillips Exeter?

Gasdsen: Yes. There's common ground, although I probably have a slightly different perspective in the sense that my prep school experience happened at a very different time and cultural place. The Civil Rights movement, for example, changed a good deal, if not everything.

Pinsker: Of course. After all, if we can agree that Holden went to Pencey in 1951, my guess would be that there were few, if any, black students at Phillips Exeter during this period.

Gasdsen: A few, but a very few.

Pinsker: There are *no* blacks at Pencey.

Gasdsen: Right.

Pinsker: Indeed, there are no blacks at any of Holden's former prep schools. He would surely have mentioned them had they been there.

Gasdsen: No question. At Exeter, we had about twenty-five black students at the time—out of a student body of 850.

Pinsker: Lorene Cary's *Black Ice* describes a similar situation. Raised in Philadelphia, Pennsylvania, she is given the opportunity to attend a prestigious prep school in New England, and what her book chronicles is the pros and cons of being thrown into a very challenging, oftentimes very difficult situation. Even many years later (she is now a successful journalist), Cary remains ambivalent. Is that pretty much how you feel?

Gasdsen: I do, too.

Pinsker: That's not beyond understanding. But sorting out the mixed feelings is what's interesting, and what finally appeals to readers who did not share the particulars of your experience. For example, at Phillips Exeter, did you notice cliques of the sort that Holden describes in *The Catcher in the Rye*?

Gasdsen: Absolutely.

Pinsker: Would you agree with Holden that most of your fellow students were "phonies"? Or is he being too harsh?

Gasdsen: That's a tough one. I'm going to say yes, but with certain qualifications. As the years go by, I've had telephone conversations with various people as I work on my book. As a result, you begin to learn things like "Yes, a lot of people *were* phony," but what's important, I think, is *why*. It's not enough to just say that they were "phony" and leave it at that.

Pinsker: Would it be fair to say of the students who *were* phonies, they all would be drawn from the white students and that none of them were among the twenty-five black students? Or would you prefer this formula—if you collect twenty-five students of any sort, some will be this and some will be that, and, yes, some will be phonies? Or how about this possibility—that on behalf of black solidarity, none of the black students you knew at Phillips Exeter were phonies?

Gasdsen: I would love to take you up on your last proposition, but it would be a lie. I met black students who were like the black people I had known earlier in life. I called one black student "Cosby in reverse": his mother was a doctor, and his father was a lawyer. This person and I had very little in common.

Pinsker: What you're talking about are class differences rather than racial ones. Indeed, it may be that class, social station, whatever, counts for much more in a prep school setting than skin color.

Gasdsen: You're right. I learned about class at Phillips Exeter. It took some distance from Exeter to realize that because I was so involved with several struggles. First, there was the struggle of being black in this white world. Little did I realize at the time that there wasn't any "white world"; this was about class. And it took some time after leaving Exeter for me to fully comprehend class issues.

Pinsker: When Holden criticizes his classmates for being materialists, even though he himself comes from money and spends it very freely during his mad weekend in Manhattan, it must gall a person who comes from very little money.

Gasdsen: No question about that. In fact, I knew a Holden type at Exeter. He tried very much to buy my friendship, and at the same time he tried to identify with me. He wasn't like the others, but he dripped money all the same.

Pinsker: Interestingly enough, students—and adults, for that matter—who feel that they're not in the inner circle often approach black people because they believe that they have something in common. Evidently, the powers that be are lined up against both parties. I don't think that ultimately works, though.

Gasdsen: No. What this does is short-circuit any possibility of one person meeting another on an individual basis. At the same time, though, I'm happy and proud of my experience at Exeter. I learned how to write and how to speak correctly. Indeed, it was almost an embarrassment of riches—the sports facilities, the grounds, the teachers, the general ambience. It was wonderful, and I was privileged to be a part of it. I know that it was my experiences at Exeter that set me on the right path.

Pinsker: But surely those good experiences must also have come with a heavy cost.

Gasdsen: Yes, and that's where my ambivalence comes in, because I had at least two minds about what was happening to me. Now, I'm glad because I can go anywhere—back to my old stomping grounds in Harrisburg or up to Cambridge—and I know how to speak and how to fit in. This wasn't always the case. And while it may be true that Exeter hopes its graduates will end up in the board-rooms of giant corporations, I'm happy that I developed an independent way of thinking and a lifelong fascination with reading and learning. I hope to say more, much more, about this in the book I'm now writing.

Edmund N. Carpenter II attended the Lawrenceville School in Lawrenceville, New Jersey, from 1935 to 1939. He did his undergraduate work at Princeton University, followed by Harvard Law School. After a stint in the armed forces, Carpenter began his law practice in Wilmington, Delaware, where he still resides. From 1954 until 1974, he was a trustee of the Lawrenceville School.

INTERVIEW WITH EDMUND N. CARPENTER II (1998)

Pinsker: When did you first read *The Catcher in the Rye*?

Carpenter: When it first came out . . . I believe in 1951.

Pinsker: Do you remember your reaction to it?

Carpenter: I thought it was an outstanding book, one of the finest of its kind. I think it was probably the best book I had read up to that point, or since for that matter.

Pinsker: When you were a trustee of the Lawrenceville School, and there was a student who behaved as Holden does, wouldn't you have given him the boot?

Carpenter: Well, you know trustees really don't get into that. They set broad policy for the school and while they might review the number of disciplinary cases, they wouldn't be involved in individual ones.

Pinsker: I guess what I'm trying to get to is this: you loved the book, so does that mean you loved Holden?

Carpenter: Yes. I thought he was a free spirit. But you're going back a great number of years.

Pinsker: How similar were your experiences at Lawrenceville compared to the prep school ethos of Salinger's book?

Carpenter: I don't think they were very similar. After all, Holden was a very free spirit. I would like to think that I was as much a free spirit as he, but I doubt it. He was a very original thinker, willing to reevaluate conventional or traditional values, and to work things out for himself. I'd like to think of myself that way, but I don't think I was.

Pinsker: Most students when you were at school, and certainly most students, according to Holden, were really one version of phony or another. Does that strike you as accurate to your experience?

Carpenter: No. But I think there were certainly a number of them who were phony, just as there are a number of adults who are phony.

Pinsker: Holden thought that *all* adults were phony.

Carpenter: Well, I didn't, and I don't. But I do think there are a certain number of important adults who are phony.

Pinsker: Your years at Lawrenceville must have been pleasant if you came back to serve as one of the school's trustees.

Carpenter: My first year at Lawrenceville was pretty miserable. I was the victim of bullies, and so I was pretty much pushed around. I was unhappy—not homesick exactly, but relatively unhappy, looking back on it now. But the next two years were great. At that time there was not the enormous struggle, as there is today, to get into a good college. And, in fact, the selection process for prep schools was entirely different then. I, for example, never went to Lawrenceville to see it before I applied. And the same thing was true of Princeton. I just moved from my room at Lawrenceville to my room at Princeton. Most students now visit six or seven prep schools before they make up their minds, and I hear that the number of visitations is even larger when they go about choosing a college.

Pinsker: How do you account for the fact that *The Catcher in the Rye* remains so popular among students who are very different from the classmates, and world, you remember?

Carpenter: You're in a far better position than I to judge that, but it's an extremely good book about an extremely interesting—and original—young man. And he continues to be interesting for students today. After all, the revolt against authority, against institutions, has certainly grown since Holden's day, and it's now a more popular, more understood, view even that it was in 1951. So, I would expect that it would remain popular, or even get more popular today.

PREP SCHOOL CATALOGS

School catalogs are an effort to inform as well as to advertise, and the Peddie School catalog for the 1950–1951 academic year is no exception. As with all ads, one reads these glowing accounts with a certain amount of skepticism, although not perhaps with the heavy dose that Holden brings to the promotional material about Pencey Prep: "They [Pencey] advertise in about a thousand magazines, always showing some hotshot guy on a horse jumping over a fence. . . . And underneath the guy on the horse's picture, it always says: 'Since 1888 we have been molding boys into splendid, clear-thinking young men.' Strictly for the birds" (6).

The excerpts we've chosen from the Peddie School catalog provide a flavor of what schools like the imaginary Pencey looked like and how they were structured. No doubt some students must have shared Holden's displeasure, although others probably warmed to many aspects of its sport-and-study regimen. Such schools were surely in the business of preparing their graduates not only for success in college but also in the competition called Life. Despite the criticism one can offer of such institutions, their track record speaks eloquently for itself. Here, then, in the official words of one such school, is the world that they invited prospective applicants to join.

FROM THE PEDDIE SCHOOL CATALOG (1950–1951)

PEDDIE PREPARES FOR COLLEGE AND LIFE

A Living School

For eighty-five years The Peddie School, an endowed and non-profit-making institution, has been preparing boys for college and for life. Although Peddie has all the advantages and virtues of a superior independent school, it remains uniquely democratic in philosophy and scope.

Five thousand living alumni, most of whom have gone on from Peddie to successful college careers, are the pride of the School. Peddie, a medium sized school with its 350 students, is large enough to offer all kinds of activities and to present democratic living, yet small enough to give each boy individual guidance and attention.

Our Heritage

Peddie began in 1864, and its growth has been both remarkable and steady. From small beginnings and great hopes have come the present buildings and campus. Year by year the plant has been enlarged. The School today is a monument to the vision and tenacity of purpose of many who have believed so firmly in the advantages of a democratic, Christian, private preparatory school that they have been willing to sacrifice to make Peddie possible.

Our Aims

Three aims dominate the life of faculty and students at Peddie: the enrichment of the mind so that each boy may have his full share of the heritage of the past and be carefully grounded for college; the development of character, without which learning may actually be dangerous; the growth of personality so that the potentialities of the individual may be realized.

Our Faculty

No school can rise above the level of its faculty. The teaching staff at Peddie is the product of many years of building. It is an experienced faculty. Its members have been chosen carefully, and changes are made infrequently. The average service to the School of its masters is more than a decade. Here are Christian gentlemen, masters in their field, who love boys and who know how to prepare them for college and life. The Peddie boy becomes a member of a great family in which he works, plays, and shares the intimacies of life with men who, by sympathetic understanding, bring out the best in him. Peddie's faculty do not represent any particular section; rather they are outstanding men from the best colleges in the United States.

Individual Attention

The success of The Peddie School is based on the effectiveness of its unique plan of focusing attention upon the boy as an individual. Every effort is made to understand a boy, and every member of the faculty is vitally interested in the amount of guidance and aid he can give the individual.

Planned Guidance

The Headmaster's part in such a plan is most important, for it is he who interviews a boy, who writes the detailed reports to the parents concerning a student's progress, and who best understands a boy as a member of the School. The Assistant Headmaster guides a boy's course of study through a series of conferences so that each student pursues the course of study best suited to his own needs—an individual curriculum. The Director of Guidance makes sure that each boy's adjustment to school life as well as his vocational plans are carefully considered. The Director of Extra-Curricular Activities sees that all boys participate in a well balanced group of activities.

One Adviser

Every boy has an adviser, a master chosen if possible by that boy. Although each teacher has a personal interest in all the boys, he has a small group of advisees with whom he is in even more intimate contact. His interest extends beyond the usual problems of academics and discipline into matters of personality and character. He keeps in touch with a boy and through conferences knows him well.

Small Classes

In his academic work a boy constantly receives individual attention. Small classes, which average nine pupils, give each boy the opportunity to recite several times each period. At the conclusion of each day is a full period Special Help class at which a boy may receive individual aid.

Reliable Measurements

Each boy's ability and achievement are tested in conformity with the most modern testing devices, such as those offered by the Educational Records Bureau. The American Psychological Test is given annually, and the Cooperative tests in specific subjects are used to check standards and to register progress. Reading and arithmetic tests are presented each fall; for those boys for whom it seems wise, remedial work in those subjects is required.

General Course

While Peddie is primarily a college preparatory institution, provision is made for boys where experience proves that college should not be their objective. This is determined on the basis of ability tests and scholastic achievement in the School. For such boys there is a special department which plans a program leading to graduation with a general diploma. These boys at graduation will have received a worthwhile cultural basis for happy and successful living.

DAILY SCHEDULE

Following is a typical day's schedule at Peddie:

7:10	Rising bell	11:50	Classes end
7:30	Breakfast	12:05	Lunch
8:30	Chapel	1:20	Afternoon classes begin
9:00	Classes start	2:40	Classes end

3:15	Special help period ends	8:00	Evening study period
3:40	Recreation	9:00	Lights out—lower school
6:00	Dinner	10:20	Lights out—underclassmen
6:45	Activity period	11:00	Lights out—seniors

On Wednesdays and Saturdays there is a half-holiday for scheduled athletic events and recreation.

OUTFIT

Equipment for Room

Every student should be provided with six sheets, blankets for a single bed, a pillow and six pillow cases, two bureau scarves, hand and bath towels, and toilet articles. If the student does not furnish bedding, a charge of $25 for the school year is made for the use of same. Each boy when registered is assigned a laundry number, marking tapes for which will be forwarded from the School. Every article of clothing and all other articles which may need laundering must be plainly marked with this tape. Boys furnish their own rugs, window draperies, floor lamps, etc.

Clothing for Dress and Sports

In addition to ordinary clothing for the school year, each boy should also be provided with a pair of stout shoes, storm rubbers or galoshes, a raincoat, a bathrobe, slippers, and clothing suitable for play and outdoor sports such as touch football, softball, tennis, and golf. Students need to furnish their own athletic footwear, gloves, sticks, racquets, etc. The School otherwise equips all members of inter-scholastic teams. If a boy wears glasses, he should have at least one duplicate pair.

AN ALTERNATIVE PREP SCHOOL EXPERIENCE

Like Nate Gasdsen, Lorene Cary was an African American high school student who was given the opportunity to prep at the formerly all-white, all-male environs of the elite St. Paul's School in New Hampshire. What the school has in mind in nothing less than a rigorous "boot camp" that will allow African American students to become future leaders. The project in social engineering, however, does not come without considerable cost—something that the teachers, administrators, and student body of St. Paul's had not reckoned on. Cary is determined to succeed, but without "selling out." But in a world where failing calculus or winning a student election could each be viewed as a betrayal of one's skin, ambivalence becomes Cary's dominant theme. True, St. Paul's prepared her with a career in journalism, and that required merciless drilling in standard English; but it also created a double role that she explores in the metaphor of "black ice," the thin coating on winter roads that can be as deceptive as it is dangerous. Cary's memoir also explores the universal themes of a young woman's confusing adolescence, and in this sense the book provides an intriguing counterpoint to Holden Caulfield's male perspective.

FROM LORENE CARY, *BLACK ICE*
(New York: Vintage, 1991)

The First Night Service took place, according to tradition on the first day of each term since the nineteenth century, in the Old Chapel. . . . Unlike the grand New Chapel, this church was small and homey. It did not dwarf or intimidate us.

In the Old Chapel my mind flipped through its familiar images of pious devotion: the Jesus, blond and bland, wispy beard and wistful eyes, who had smiled at me from over my great-grandparents' bed, from the Sunday-school room at Ward A.M.E., from the illuminated cross over the pulpit, and from cardboard fans and free calendars produced by black funeral parlors; the brunet Jesus who stretched his arms out toward his disciples at the Last Supper in my laminated reproduction of Leondardo da Vinci's oil. *Take, eat.*

The Rector appeared in the pulpit, shorter than he had seemed in the

Rectory, and businesslike. I heard him, despite the close intimacy of the chapel, as if he were speaking from far away. . . . He talked to us of our fears and our dreams, of our new career, of the challenges of our life together.

Then he spoke of tradition. Boys had come and gone before us, sitting in these same pews, thinking and feeling these same thoughts and feelings. They had grown into men and gone out into the world prepared, by a St. Paul's education, to do something worthwhile.

My own voices were talking back to him, and so long as he spoke, I could not control the dialogue. Part of the tradition, my eye. I was there in spite, despite, *to* spite it. I was there because of sit-ins and marches and riots. I was there—and this I felt with extraordinary and bitter certainty—as a sort of liberal-minded experiment.

PREP SCHOOLS IN OTHER FICTIONAL WORKS

Literally dozens of novels about troubled adolescents were mar-
keted as new versions of *The Catcher in the Rye*; most of them
were clearly inferior goods. One exception, however, is John
Knowles's *A Separate Peace* (1960). Set in the Devon School (read:
Phillips Exeter) during the early years of World War II, much of its
plotline revolves around the relationship between two students—
Gene and Phineas. Gene is the loner intellectual, as introverted as
he is sensitive, while Phineas is cast as a handsome, daredevil ath-
lete. The arithmetic of their complicated friendship is played out
against the backdrop of Devon, and that is where the comparisons
with Salinger's novel seem most appropriate—for Knowles captures, as few novels in the post-*Catcher* period do, the dailiness of
daily life at a prep school.

FROM JOHN KNOWLES, *A SEPARATE PEACE*
(New York: Macmillan, 1960)

Saturday afternoons are terrible in a boys' school, especially in the winter.
There is no football game; it is not possible, as it is in the spring, to take
bicycle trips into the surrounding country. Not even the most grinding
student can feel required to lose himself in his books, since there is
Sunday ahead, long, lazy, quiet Sunday, to do any homework.

And these Sundays are worst in the late winter when the snow has lost
its novelty and its shine, and the school seems to have been reduced to
only a network of drains. During the brief thaw in the early afternoon
there is a dismal gurgling of dirty water seeping down pipes and along
gutters, a gray seamy shifting beneath the crust of snow, which cracks to
show patches of frozen mud beneath. Shrubbery loses its bright snow
headgear and stands bare and frail, too undernourished to hide the
drains it was intended to hide. These are the days when going into any
building you cross a mat of dirt and cinders led in by others before you.
The sky is an empty hopeless gray and gives the impression that this is
its eternal shade. Winter's occupation seems to have conquered, overrun
and destroyed everything, so that now there is no longer any resistance
movement left to nature; all the juices are dead, every sprig of vitality
snapped, and now winter itself, an old, corrupt, tired conqueror, loosens

its grip on the desolation, recedes a little, grows careless in its watch; sick of victory and enfeebled by the absences of challenge, it begins itself to withdraw from the ruined countryside. The drains alone are active, and on these Saturdays their noises sound a dull recessional to winter.

A SCHOLARLY LOOK AT PREP SCHOOLS

Peter W. Cookson, Jr. and Caroline Hodges Persell's *Preparing for Power: America's Elite Boarding Schools* takes a disinterested, scholarly look at prep schools, albeit one critical of the systematic effort to sacrifice the individual spirit to the collective will. By likening prep schools to a "crucible," they mean to call attention to an ethos that Holden, for one, staunchly resists. As you read their account of the years before and after Holden attended Pencey, think about the idyllic vision of life presented by the Peddie School catalog as well as about Holden's descriptions of rampant phonies and hypocrisy. Remember, too, that truth is likely to emerge from an attention to specific detail and that not all the details are likely to point to a single, unified judgment.

FROM PETER W. COOKSON, JR. AND CAROLINE HODGES
PERSELL, "THE PREP CRUCIBLE," IN *PREPARING FOR POWER: AMERICA'S ELITE BOARDING SCHOOLS*
(New York: Basic Books, 1985)

Likening prep schools to crucibles may seem incongruous or exaggerated. After all, most prep schools look more like playgrounds than industrial blast furnaces, and coolness, not heat, is the popular perception of prep style. However, the crucible metaphor is more apt than it might at first appear, for since their inception the elite schools have had the responsibility of melting down the refractory material of individualism into the solid metal of elite collectivism. By isolating students from their home world and intervening in their development, it is hoped that they will become soldiers for their class. A good many soldiers, however, also run the risk of being prisoners of their class. The total institution is a moral milieu where pressure is placed on individuals to give up significant parts of their selves to forward the interests of the group. As one admissions officer said, "We don't want selfish learners here." What should be remembered is that while outward conformity is required, more importantly, treatment is designed to penetrate deep below the surface of student behavior into their very consciousness, so that values and even somatic needs are subject to standardization and regulation. Thus, the requirement that students eat, sleep, and study together creates and continuously reinforces a sense of collective identity. As we shall see, at one girls school, the students all sleep together on a sleeping porch, virtually eliminating any sense of privacy.

The fledgling prep school student embarks on a "moral career" that is difficult and complex. Much of the socialization that goes on in prep schools is done by other students. They teach each other how to dress, think, and often what and how to study. They also share alcohol and drugs, and protect each other by a code of silence. Giving information to the administration that is detrimental to one's peers is considered a form of treason by nearly all prep school students.

While many students report that they found their prep school experience rewarding and positive, too many report that their experiences have made them cynical and unhappy not to conclude that the prep crucible does take a toll. Caught between the demands of parents, school, and peers, prep school students are forced daily to make decisions about life and themselves that are immediate and often poignant.

As the previous selection indicates, prep schools operate from a set of assumptions about the individual and the group; the necessity of molding students to assume leadership roles in the future; and perhaps most of all, the enforcement, both consciously and unconsciously, of certain cultural codes. With regard to the last item, we have included an excerpt from an essay by American Studies professor Christopher Brookeman because it places prep school "codes" within a larger context, one that found rich expression in David Riesman's sociological study *The Lonely Crowd* and that permeated a good many films and popular songs during the latter years of the 1950s. Granted, Holden fought his lonely battles with authority and conformity before the culture itself caught up with him, but we felt it worth putting this material before you if only to raise questions about whether or not Holden's attitudes are a harbinger of things to come. Is he the quintessential "rebel" before 1950s-style rebels appeared on the scene?

We chose the Brookeman essay for other reasons as well. It is a good model of close reading enhanced by an application to a wider context. As you read through the arguments, you are likely to find places where you agree and, indeed, where you had thought much the same thing yourself, as well as places where his references are unfamiliar and the conclusions he draws from them perhaps unclear. In the first case, think of the experience as a confidence-builder; in the second, use what you *don't* know as an occasion that regular visits to the library can rectify.

FROM CHRISTOPHER BROOKEMAN, "PENCEY PREPPY:
CULTURAL CODES IN *THE CATCHER IN THE RYE*," IN *NEW
ESSAYS ON THE CATCHER IN THE RYE*
(Jack Slazman, ed. New York: Cambridge University Press, 1991)

Holden Caulfield, like Huck Finn, has become a mythic figure of adolescent rebellion in American culture. One continuing rich source for this presentation of Holden, usually as a rebel against the conformist pressures of post–Second World War American society, is the American history textbook designed for high school use. In a typical example, Daniel F. Davis and Norman Langer, authors of *A History of the United States since 1945*, argue that Holden's "adventures say a great deal about the worth of the individual in American society. They also remind readers how vulnerable every individual can be."[1]

. . .

The cult status of Holden as a generalized champion of American individualism and indicator of the psychic disturbances caused by the stresses of postindustrial society is evident not only in the world of high school textbooks. In a book by the cultural critic Christopher Lasch, *Haven in a Heartless World: The Family Besieged* (1977), we find the following assessment of the seminal status of Holden as a weathervane for the various anxieties that have developed within the nuclear family as parental authority has declined in modern America:

> Films, comic strips, and popular novels—in particular the many novels of adolescent revolt, patterned after J. D. Salinger's "The Catcher in the Rye"—ridicule the "manifest" father, and authority in general, while depicting "latent" father-figures as sinister, aggressive, and utterly unprincipled in their persecution of their hero or heroine.[3]

By turning Holden into a symptom of a general cultural malaise, critics have failed to give attention to the fact that Salinger locates Holden's story within a very specific social world in which the most significant influence is not some generalized concept of American culture or society, but the codes and practices of a particular instrument of social control—the American prep school. Even when the action moves to New York, Holden stays, in the main, within a finely tuned collegiate culture of dates and movie going. This is clear from his description of the sociology of the clientele in a Greenwich Village nightclub named after the resident pianist: "Even though it was so late, old Ernie's was jam-packed, mostly with prep school jerks and college jerks."[4] It is within the immediate, primary context of Pencey Prep, where we first encounter Holden, that we need to situate all the agencies that seek to influence his development, such as the peer group, parents, and the mass media. Only then will we do justice to J. D. Salinger's portrait of the anxiety-ridden adolescent within the particular faction of the middle class whose behavior and psychology are the substance of *The Catcher in the Rye*.

NOTES

1. Daniel F. Davis and Norman Langer, *A History of the United States since 1945* (New York: Scholastic, 1987), p. 71.

. . .

3. Christopher Lasch, *Haven in a Heartless World: The Family Besieged* (New York: Basic Books, 1977), p. 176.

4. J. D. Salinger, *The Catcher in the Rye* (New York: Bantam, 1964), p. 83. All subsequent page references, appearing in parentheses in the text, are to this edition.

STUDY QUESTIONS

1. How much does Holden's prep school experience influence the relationship he has with his teachers?

2. Compare Holden's interaction with his teachers to your interaction with your teachers.

3. Critics often characterize Holden as a universal teenager. However, only a small percentage of American teenagers go to prep schools. Determine if you think the critics are correct by citing passages from the novel.

4. There are a number of examples of the kind of education Holden has received throughout *The Catcher in the Rye*. Analyze the quality of this education compared to your high school education.

5. Athletics play an important role at Pencey Prep. Using Holden as an example support or condemn that role.

6. Compare the role of athletics at Pencey Prep with the athletic program at your school.

7. Prep school students are often stereotyped as snobby. Analyze Holden's behaviors in terms of this image. Holden would balk at any characterization of this sort. If Holden had to justify his behaviors to "prove" he wasn't a snob, what examples would he give?

8. Comment on the statement that Holden would be a misfit and a rebel regardless of the setting.

9. According to Ian Hamilton, Salinger's nickname at Valley Forge Academy was "Salinger the Sublime." Think of a nickname Holden's classmates might have given him.

10. In some respects Ian Hamilton's article represents Salinger to be just the kind of "phony" Holden often mentions. Assess the validity of this statement.

11. Examine the excerpts on the "Living School" and "Aims" from the Peddie School Catalog. Compare them to the goals and aims of your school.

12. According to "The Prep Crucible" students embark on "moral careers" when they enter prep schools. Assess this statement in terms of Holden's career at Pencey.

13. David Riesman considers Holden a rebel in our "other-directed" society. Using Christopher Brookeman's article and examples from *The Catcher in the Rye*, agree or disagree with Riesman's statement.

TOPICS FOR WRITTEN OR ORAL EXPLORATION

1. In 1873 James McCosh proposed a network of college preparatory schools that would include the best elements of the English "public schools." Research the English public school system and compile a list of the elements that American schools should adopt. Describe any characteristics of the English public school system that you think would not work in the United States.

2. Using Ian Hamilton's excerpt, compare Holden's experience at Pencey Prep to J. D. Salinger's experience at Valley Forge Academy.

3. Imagine you are Holden's father. The headmaster at Pencey Prep is asking why you want your son to be admitted to the school. How would you respond?

4. Read the excerpt from *In Search of J. D. Salinger* and imagine that you are writing about a grown-up Holden Caulfield. Ask Holden's former classmates the same questions Ian Hamilton asked J. D. Salinger's former classmates. Respond to those questions as you think they would.

5. Use Ian Hamilton's article to determine if there is any correspondence between how Holden characterizes his teachers and J. D. Salinger's relationship to his teachers.

6. Salinger wrote his class history for the Valley Forge yearbook when he was a senior. If Holden had this assignment, what do you think he might have said?

7. Create a guide for your ideal school starting with its aims of providing the students with the type of education that you think would most benefit students of today.

8. One of the questions in our society is if tax relief should be allowed for parents who send their children to private schools. Prepare an argument that you would use as the parent of children in the public schools if you were appearing before a congressional hearing on the matter. Then prepare a response as if you were a parent of private school students.

9. Many critics contend prep schools encourage snobbery. Write an editorial taking one side of that issue. When you have completed it, write a letter to the editor in response to that editorial, taking the opposite view.

10. Consider the daily schedule from the Peddie School Catalog. Discuss if students today would benefit from a schedule of this type.

11. "The Prep Crucible" states the role of a prep school education is to create members for the upper class. Research this statement by studying the catalogs of a number of preparatory schools. Prepare a report that would support or refute this statement.

12. Compare and contrast the role of uniformity in public and private schools.

13. Compare and contrast living in dormitories versus living with families for teenagers.

14. Many public schools today are adopting one of the traditional characteristics of private and preparatory schools—the uniform. Prepare an oral argument that you would present to a school board that is considering such a move. Also prepare to answer your own argument.

SUGGESTED READINGS

The following books provide additional background to, and analysis of, preparatory schools in America.

Abramowitz, Susan, and E. Ann Stackhouse. *The Private High School Today*. Washington, D.C.: National Institute of Education, 1980.

Baird, Leonard L. *The Elite Schools*. Lexington, Mass.: Lexington Books, 1977.

Baltzell, E. Digby. *Puritan Boston and Quaker Philadelphia*. New York and London: Free Press, 1979.

Barrett, Joan, and Sally F. Goldfarb. *The Insider's Guide to Prep Schools*. New York: E. P. Dutton, 1979.

Birnbach, Lisa, ed. *The Official Preppy Handbook*. New York: Workman, 1980.

Coles, Robert. *Children of Privilege*. Boston: Little, Brown, 1977.

Erickson, Donald A., and Richard L. Nault. *Characteristics and Relationships in Public and Private Schools*. San Francisco: Center for Research on Private Education, University of San Francisco, 1979.

Gossage, Carolyn. *A Question of Privilege*. Toronto: Peter Martin, 1977.

Halberstam, David. *The Best and the Brightest*. New York: Random House, 1969.

Kraushaur, Otto F. *Private Schools: From the Puritans to the Present*. Bloomington, Ill.: Phi Beta Kappa Educational Foundation, 1976.

McLachlan, James. *American Boarding Schools: A Historical Study*. New York: Charles Scribner's Sons, 1970.

Riesman, David. *The Lonely Crowd: A Study of the Changing American Character*. Rev. ed. New Haven, Conn.: Yale University Press, 1970.

Spring, Joel. *The Sorting Machine*. New York: David McKay, 1976.

Wakeford, John. *The Cloistered Elite*. New York: Praeger, 1969.

5

Holden Caulfield at the Movies

In the opening page of *The Catcher in the Rye*, Holden makes it clear that he hates movies. The remark is prompted not only by his disappointment that his brother, D. B., a writer whose early short stories he much admires, has chucked a serious literary life for the siren call of Hollywood but also because the movies corrupt those who watch them. Interestingly enough, Ernest Hemingway had much the same reaction. In a sketch entitled "On Writing" (included in *The Nick Adams Stories* [1972]), he has Nick Adams, his fictional mouthpiece, make the following observation: *"The movies ruined everything. Like talking about something good. That was what had made the war unreal. Too much talking."* But while Hemingway and Salinger are of similar minds about the movies, it is also clear that they are quite different in personality and temperament. As a solider in World War II, Salinger presumably met the world-famous Hemingway during one of the latter's stints as a war correspondent. By this time Hemingway was a bloated parody of his former self: the leaner, hungrier writer whose early stories changed the rhythms of American prose forever. When he grabbed the celebrity spotlight by shooting the heads off a couple of chickens, Salinger was appalled.

Nonetheless, the young Salinger is thought to have handed the older writer a couple of his short stories. To paraphrase the concluding lines of Hemingway's *The Sun Also Rises* (1926), it would be "pretty to think" that this exchange actually took place, especially since one could then argue that the two most influential collections of American short stories, Hemingway's *In Our Time* (1925) and Salinger's *Nine Stories* (1965), were related biographically. What we do know, however, is that, after the war, Salinger wrote Hemingway a letter in which he talked about working on a play about a character named Holden Caulfield. The larger point, however, is that the case for influence assumes that the literary world operates as a race in which one runner/writer exchanges the baton with another. This is not generally the case because "influence," however one defines this slippery term, is much more complicated. What remains uncontested, however, is the fact that both Hemingway and Salinger had deep reservations about the world according to Hollywood.

Granted, Hemingway could count many of Hollywood's movers and shakers among his close personal friends: director John Ford and actors Gary Cooper and Marlene Dietrich. By contrast, Salinger has retained his skepticism. No film version of *The Catcher in the Rye* has been made, nor, so far as we know, is any in the works. Indeed, there are good reasons to believe that any efforts to option the novel (and it is hard to believe that many weren't tossed his way) were immediately squelched. For Hemingway, the movies ruined things because they talked about matters that were best savored *un*stated. Much preferring the sensuous detail of ice-cold mountain streams and the ritualized way in which true fishermen go about their business, Hemingway distrusted abstractions. Moreover, he felt (rightly) that many writers expressed emotions they *thought* they should have, rather than the ones they actually did. Hemingway's manifesto consisted of nothing more or less than a commitment to the simple declarative sentence that was "true." Movies were interested in quite other things: illusion, fakery, and, most important of all, large box-office receipts.

For Holden, movies were, in his all-purpose word, *phony*. But just as Holden's large (self-righteous) proclamations do not always square with his actions, so, too, does his ranting about the corrupting influence of movies. He simply knows too much about what he attacks and protests too much about not being at least partially formed by the Hollywood dream factory.

What sort of movies might Holden have seen? The text makes it clear that Laurence Olivier's 1948 version of *Hamlet* would be one, along with enough Warner Brothers gangster flicks featuring Edward G. Robinson, James Cagney, or Humphrey Bogart to give him a pretty good idea of how on-screen tough guys live and die. Holden is lukewarm about Olivier's stellar performance as Hamlet, but the gestures and attitudes of movie tough guys added a measure of sophisticated wit to his very nonheroic self. This is particularly true in the moments after Stradlater decked him, and Holden needs a way to save whatever face he can. Still, there are enough melancholy brooding and interior questions to think of Holden as a version of Hamlet, albeit one who speaks his soliloquies in teen-age idioms. If Holden doesn't see the connection between himself and the introspective Hamlet, his author did—for that was surely why he inserted impressions of *Hamlet* into his novel.

As with the history of baseball, the history of Hollywood films tells us a good deal about America—especially during the decades when movies did not have to compete with television for large audiences. People went to movie theaters in droves, partly because the price of a ticket was relatively cheap, partly because movie theaters had air-conditioning long before many other public places or private homes, and partly because Hollywood films served up various slices of the American Dream. Movies, in short, offered audiences a chance to experience another person's experiences— sometimes as historical (and heroic) figures such as the scientist Madame Curie, the British prime minister Benjamin Disraeli, or the American president Abraham Lincoln, who all helped to mold public values.

As an uncompromising social critic, Holden entered movie theaters with popcorn in one hand and suspicion in the other. There are good reasons to feel that Salinger felt roughly the same way, although we do not know what films he did, or did not, see. Probably not many, but he certainly was acquainted with the musical extravaganzas that offered an escape from, and a temporary alternative to, the grinding poverty of the Great Depression: *Forty-second Street* (1933), *Gold Diggers of 1933* (1933), *Flying Down to Rio* (1933), and, not least of all, *The Great Ziegfeld* (1936). The last film is especially noteworthy because Holden is too young to have attended performances of the *Ziegfeld's Follies*, a stage show that was a combination of vaudeville and Broadway musicals made famous by producer Florenz Ziegfeld. Salinger has probably gathered many of his impressions from the film about Ziegfeld's career.

It sported an all-star cast introduced by Dick Powell as Florenz Ziegfeld in heaven and highlighting the following: a Fanny Brice–Hume Cronyn comedy sketch, a Fred Astaire–Gene Kelly dance, comedian Red Skelton's "Guzzler's Gin sketch," Lena Horne's singing solo, and Judy Garland's "The Interview" sketch. Others in the cast included Lucille Ball and Cyd Charisse. Filmed mostly in 1944, various segments were directed by Roy Del Ruth, Norman Taurog, Lemuel Ayers, Robert Lewis, and Merrill Pye.

Moreover, Holden's impromptu performance in the bathroom (while Stradlater shaves for his date with Jane Gallagher) is a blending of the hokey plots one finds in depression-era films such as *Forty-second Street* or the Gold Diggers's series (for example, a young chorus girl replaces an injured or otherwise ailing star and becomes an overnight success) and the alternating rhythms of Holden's attraction/repulsion. Well aware that he is no tap dancer, he points out that the bathroom's stone floor makes a great tap surface, especially if one has seen enough Hollywood musicals to give them a parodic spin. Holden launches into an elaborate imitation in which he is the governor's son, and his father doesn't want him to be a dancer (by this time the connections to Holden's own situation are clear). But there he is, tap dancing away, when the lead turns up drunk, and Holden has to fill the breach. To be sure, Holden realizes that this is a corny scenario, but it is also one that gives him more pleasure than he likes to admit.

For Holden, motion pictures may be "lousy," but they are better than sitting in the dormitory feeling depressed. Even more to the point, when it turns out that Mal Brossard and Ackley have already seen the one flick playing at Agerstown, Holden can barely hide his disappointment. Despite being an adolescent who looks down his nose at popular culture, he is, at least partially, a product of its enormous cultural influence.

Consider, for example, the scene in which Holden imagines himself as a dying gangster, his gut full of lead from a barrage by Federal Bureau of Investigation (FBI) agents. Granted, his colorful imagination wildly exaggerates the antiheroic truth, namely, that Maurice, the elevator operator/pimp, has punched him in the stomach, and Holden needs to regain what control he can by shifting reality into another, more theatrical dimension. First, he imagines that he has a bullet in his gut: Maurice shot him, and Holden pretends that he has gone to the bathroom for a stiff belt of bourbon, anything to steady his nerves and allow him to spring into action. The way Holden figures it, he will come out of the bathroom a more or less new man, he will get dressed, and, with a pistol in his pocket, he will go about the business of taking his revenge—staggering just enough for a full melodramatic effect.

Ultimately, Holden imagines making his way to the elevator and ringing the bell. When Maurice notices the automatic in Holden's hand, he begins to beg for his life in his "high-pitched, yellow-belly voice," but Holden plugs him anyway: "Six shots right through his fat hairy belly." Of such fantasies is consolation made—albeit, of a decidedly limited sort. Holden doesn't have a particular gangster flick in mind but rather a pastiche of the genre. *The Public Enemy* (1931), *Scarface* (1932), and *High Sierra* (1941). According to a 1931 issue of *Movie Star News*, gangster films "surpass westerns at the box office," with James Cagney's role in *The Public Enemy* as "the first to portray gangsters as the spawn of social problems."

THE GANGSTER FILM GENRE

In order to properly discuss the movies of Holden's culture and analyze their influence on him, the director Daryl Zanuck needs to be introduced. According to Carlos Clarens, author of *Crime Movies* (1980), a definitive survey of the gangster film genre from silent filmmaker D. W. Griffith to Mario Puzo's *The Godfather* trilogy, Zanuck was given a very small budget (because Jack L. Warner, head of Warner Brothers studio, had little enthusiasm for gangster films), but he managed to bring in three films that changed American viewing habits forever: *Doorway to Hell* (1930), *Little Caesar* (1930), and *The Public Enemy* (1931):

> All three pictures told basically the same story, that of the rise and fall of a gangster. They shared the drab Warner look of the period, and many of their characters appeared interchangeable; yet a style was clearly taking form from picture to picture, almost independently of their directors.

If it is true that sensationalistic accounts of urban criminals were a staple of the popular press and that the "truth" about gangsters had an influence on filmmakers, it is even truer that Hollywood added many wrinkles of its own. The tough talk and menacing gestures we associate with Humphrey Bogart, James Cagney, and Edward G. Robinson set the gold standard for decades of future tough guys who, like Holden, learned the "right moves" by going to the movies.

FROM MORDAUNT HALL, "REVIEW OF *LITTLE CAESAR*"
(*New York Times*, January 10, 1931)

"Little Caesar," based on W. R. Burnett's novel of Chicago gangdom, was welcomed to the Strand yesterday by unusual crowds. The story deals with the career of Cesare Bandello, alias Rico, alias Little Caesar, a disagreeable lad who started by robbing gasoline stations and soared to startling heights in his "profession" by reason of his belief in his high destiny.

FROM A.D.S., "REVIEW OF *THE PUBLIC ENEMY*"
(*New York Times*, April 21, 1931)

It is just another gangster film at the Strand, weaker than most in its story, stronger than most in its acting, and like most maintaining a certain level of interest through the last burst of machine-gun fire. . . .

There is a prologue apprising the audience that the hoodlums and terrorists of the underworld must be exposed and the glamour ripped from them. There is an epilogue pointing out the moral that civilization is on her knees and inquiring loudly as to what is to be done. And before the prologue there is a brief stage tableau, with sinuous green lighting which shows a puppet gangster shooting another puppet gangster in the back.

"The Public Enemy" does not, as its title so eloquently suggests, present a picture of the war between the underworld and the upperworld. Instead the war is one of gangsters among themselves; of sensational and sometimes sensational incoherent murders. The motivation is lost in the general slaughter at the end, when Matt and Tom, the hoodlums with whose career of outlawry the picture is concerned, die violently.

Edward Woods and James Cagney, as Matt and Tom respectively, give remarkably lifelike portrayals of young hoodlums. The story follows their careers from boyhood, through the war period and into the early days of prohibition, when the public thirst made their peculiar talents profitable. Slugging disloyal bartenders, shooting down rival beermen, slapping their women crudely across the face, strutting with a vast self-satisfaction through their little world, they contribute a hard and true picture of the unheroic gangster.

FROM MORDAUNT HALL, "REVIEW OF *SCARFACE*"
(*New York Times*, May 20, 1932)

The slaughter in "Scarface, the Shame of a Nation," the Howard Hughes gangster production . . . is like that of a Shakespearean tragedy for after the smoke of machine guns and pineapple bombs has blown away and the leading killer has gone to his death on the gallows, the only one of a group of principal characters left is a blonde with carefully plucked eyebrows—she who had been the mistress of two underworld giants.

This pictorial recapitulation . . . is a stirring picture, efficiently directed and capably acted, but as was once said of "The Covered Wagon," that it is all very well if you liked wagons, so this is an excellent diversion of those who like to take an afternoon or an evening off to study the activities of cowardly thugs.

At the onset, Tony is second in command to Lovo, played by Osgood Perkins. No sooner does he get into a tight place with the police than he is released through a habeas corpus writ. He not only has his eye on becoming No. 1, but he also reveals a liking for Lovo's girl, Poppy, impersonated by Karen Morley. He is warned by Lovo to keep away from the North Side. Lovo insists that there is plenty of business for their beer racket on the South Side, with its 30,000 saloons and half a million customers. Tony, however, takes a tourist advertising sign that reads, "The World is Yours" for his motto, and he decides to humble Lovo by disobeying orders.

FROM BOSELY CROWTHER, "REVIEW OF *HIGH SIERRA*"
(New York Times, January 29, 1941)

We wouldn't know for certain whether the twilight of the American gangster is here. But the Warner Brothers, who should know if anybody does, have apparently taken it for granted, and in a solemn Wagnerian mood are giving that titanic figure a send-off befitting a first-string god in the film called "High Sierra," which arrived yesterday at the Strand. Yes-sir, Siegfried himself never rose to more heroic heights than does Mr. Humphrey Bogart, the last of the great gunmen, when, lodged on a high mountain crag with an army of coppers below, he shouts defiantly at his tormentors ere his noble sound takes flight. It's truly magnificent, that's all.

As a matter of fact—and aside from the virtues of the film itself—it is rather touching to behold the Warners pay such a glowing tribute, for no one has made a better thing out of the legendary gangster than they have. So, indeed, we are deeply moved by this honest payment of respects to an aging and graying veteran of the Nineteen Thirty banditti who makes his last stand his best. Somehow, it seems quite fitting.

Of course, that is exactly the way the Warners and everyone concerned intended it should seem. For the story which is told is that of a notorious hold-up man who is sprung out of an Illinois prison by an old gangland pal who wants him in California for a big job.

As gangster pictures go, this one has everything—speed, excitement, suspense and that ennobling suggestion of futility which makes for irony and pity. Mr. Bogart plays the leading role with a perfection of hard-boiled vitality. . . . As gangster pictures go—if they do—it's a perfect epilogue. Count on the old guard and the Warners: they die but never surrender.

Gangster films were not the only fare that the Hollywood studio system cranked out during the period between 1931 and 1951.

There were musicals, biographical treatments, biblical epics, war flicks, detective thrillers, novels turned into films, and westerns by the wagonload. In this regard, you might see Hollywood's Dream Factory in the spirit of the game known as "Six Degrees of Kevin Bacon," but this time, played with older actors and much older films. The parlor game referred to owes its peculiar life to John Guare's 1996 play *Six Degrees of Separation*. As Guare's (comic) argument would have it, all of us are (at most) only six separations from everyone else.

At one point in the play, *The Catcher in the Rye* gets a prominent mention. "A substitute teacher out in Long Island," one character points out, "was dropped from his job for fighting with a student. A few weeks later, the teacher returned to the classroom, shot the student unsuccessfully, held the class hostage and then shot himself. This fact caught my eye: last sentence. *Times*. A neighbor described him a nice boy. Always reading *Catcher in the Rye*." That observation on the table, the talk then moves on to Mark Chapman, the assassin of John Lennon who, according to Guare's play, "did it because he wanted to draw the attention of the world to *The Catcher in the Rye* and the reading of that book would be his defense." Ditto for "young Hinckley, the whiz kid who shot Reagan and his press secretary."

Watching the play of dazzling wit that makes *Six Degrees of Separation* so enjoyable onstage (as well as in its film version), one tends to see relationships in whole new ways—including the hundreds of films that predate Holden that are nonetheless included in his dismissive judgment that they ruin everything. As for the references to *The Catcher in the Rye*, Holden Caulfield, or J. D. Salinger, they are more evidence that art and life are much more inextricably related than many might wish.

CINEMATIC ALLUSIONS IN *CATCHER*

Thus far we have been focusing on some of the film genres that find their way into Holden's ambivalent notion of the movies. There are, in addition, several spots in *The Catcher in the Rye* where he refers to specific films. For example, Holden gets a kick out of the way that Phoebe has memorized whole portions of *The 39 Steps* and can recite key lines of this thriller along with those on the silver screen—and this long before campy reenactments of cult films such as *The Rocky Horror Picture Show*. Holden wouldn't be so charitable about those self-consciously outlandish performances as he is with his sister's behavior. Phoebe, after all, is innocence personified, and when she focuses on certain aspects of a film, it is the essence of authentic charm.

With Olivier's *Hamlet*, Phoebe enjoys the stray moment when Hamlet pats his dog's head (the rest of the film soars over her head). Holden is older and more sophisticated, but his lasting impressions of the film are much closer to Phoebe's than to those at the top of Pencey's academic heap. As he puts it in a speech that provides yet another angle on why Holden feels that a film version ruins the original:

> The best part in the whole picture was when old Ophelia's brother—the one that gets in the duel with Hamlet at the very end—was going away and his father was giving him a lot of advice. While the father kept giving him a lot of advice, old Ophelia was sort of horsing around with her brother, taking his dagger out of the holster, and teasing him and all while he was trying to look interested in the bull his father was shooting. That was nice. I got a big bang out of that. . . . What I'll have to do is, I'll have to read that play. The trouble with me is, I always have to read that stuff by myself. If an actor acts it out, I hardly listen. I keep worrying about whether he's going to do something phony every minute. (107)

FROM BOSELY CROWTHER, "REVIEW OF *HAMLET*"
(*New York Times*, September 29, 1948)

It may come as something of a rude shock to the theatre's traditionalists to discover that Shakespeare can be eloquently presented on the screen.

So bound have these poetic dramas been to the culture of our stage that the very thought of their transference may have staggered a few profound die-hards. But the matter is settled; the filmed "Hamlet" of Laurence Olivier gives absolute proof that these classics are magnificently suited to the screen.

Indeed, this finely British-made picture . . . is probably as vivid and as clear an exposition of the doleful Dane's dilemma as modern-day play-goers have seen. And just as Olivier's ingenious and spectacular "Henry V" set out new visual limits for Shakespeare's historical plays, his "Hamlet" envisions new vistas in the great tragedies of the Bard. . . .

Just as Olivier's "Henry" took the play further away by taking it out into the open—and thereby revealed it visually—his "Hamlet" makes the play more evident by bringing it closer to you. The subtle reactions of the characters, the movements of their faces and forms, which can be so dramatically expressive and which are more or less remote on the stage, are here made emotionally incisive by their normal proximity. Coupled with beautiful acting and inspired interpretations all the way, this visual closeness to drama offers insights that are brilliant and rare. . . .

Hamlet is nobody's glass-man, and the dark and troubled workings of his mind are difficult, even for Freudians. But the openness with which he is played by Mr. Olivier in this picture makes him reasonably comprehensible. His is no cold and sexless Hamlet. He is a solid and virile young man, plainly tormented by the anguish and horror of a double shock.

Oliver's *Hamlet* owed much to the writings of Ernst Jones, an American disciple of Freud. To greatly simplify his argument, Jones advanced the following oedipal thesis: Hamlet's difficulty in killing his murderous uncle represents a split between his conscious and unconscious self. On one level, he means to act as an avenger; on another, he secretly wished for his father's death because he would then have no rival for his mother's affections. Holden would have been deeply skeptical about such notions, although a fair case can be made for the ways in which Holden shares what Crowther calls Hamlet's "disillusion in women." Granted, Jane Gallagher is no Ophelia, nor is Sally Hayes, for that matter; but Holden brings roughly the same insistence about innocence to these characters as does Hamlet to his mother.

Olivier's film—as those currently being done by Kenneth Branaugh—give Shakespeare's plays a very wide (and interesting) public exposure. But to the child of well-heeled Manhattan sophisticates, theater comes with the territory, along with much else that Holden writes off as phony. Add the Lunts (Alfred Lunt and Lynn Fontanne), the premier Broadway theater couple of the time, and the stage of Salinger's novel is set for yet another of Holden's classic put-downs: "I don't like any shows very much, if you want to know the truth. They're not as bad as movies, but they're certainly nothing to rave about. In the first place, I hate actors. They never act like people. They just think they do" (107). As with many of Holden's aesthetic judgments, he is dead wrong about *I Know My Love*, the play that he takes a much-impressed Sally Hayes to see. As she puts it, in ways that raise Holden's hackles: "The Lunts! Oh, marvelous!"

What Holden fails to appreciate is everything that the Lunts epitomized: brilliant technique, inexhaustible energy, and a string of hits packed into nearly fifty years of nonstop performances. No doubt Holden likens them to Old Ernie, the Village jazz pianist who became more concerned with his fame than with his performances. The difference is that Ernie is a composite, while the Lunts and *I Know My Love* were very real. Not surprisingly, Sally thinks of them as "angels," while Holden filters what he sees onstage through his own tangled condition. Put another way, Sally is a phony because she dishes the same sort of small talk that one often hears in theater lobbies; by contrast, Holden not only speaks for himself but also speaks in vernacular appropriate to his age:

> The show wasn't as bad as some I've seen. It was on the crappy side, though. It was about five hundred thousand years in the life of this one old couple. It starts out when they're young and all, and the girl's parents don't want her to marry the boy, but she marries him anyway. The husband goes to war and the wife has this brother that's a drunkard. I couldn't get very interested. I mean I didn't care too much when anybody in the family died or anything. They were all just a bunch of actors. (114)

The Fabulous Lunts, Jared Brown's definitive biography of the theatrical couple, describes *I Know My Love* rather differently: as he saw it, the 1949 play gave the Lunts a unique opportunity "to portray the same characters at different periods of their lives, from adolescence to old age, in the portrait of a fifty-year marriage. The story would be told out of chronological order, beginning in 1939 (when the couple was celebrating their fiftieth wedding anniversary), then returning to 1888 (when they were courting) and then moving forward in time from 1902 to 1920" (Brown, *The Fabulous Lunts*, 329). S. N. Behrman, an old friend of the Lunts and author of *I Know My Love*, saw the play as a "parable of their own marriage."

FROM BROOKS ATKINSON, "REVIEW OF *I KNOW MY LOVE*"
(*New York Times*, November 3, 1941)

Although the Lunts are dazzling actors, it is difficult not to look at what they are playing. It is "I Know My Love," which S. N. Behrman has adapted from Marcel Achard's "Aupres de Ma Blonde." . . .

This is the comedy in which the Lunts appear as fabulously old people in the first act, and then begin life over at a tender age in the second act and age by easy stages for the rest of the evening. "Tour de force" is the cultured phrase generally applied to such stage antics. . . .

But let's face the facts even on the silver anniversary of the Lunts' first appearance as a team. "I Know My Love" abuses the privilege of being light. It has nothing to say and very little to contribute to entertainment. It is the life story of two persons who love each other devotedly but accumulate the usual burdens of family, the unusual burden of economic success and all the familiar irritations. Since it was by men it gallantly presents the little lady as the one who understands everything and everyone through intuition and saves the marriage in its thirtieth year by cunning manipulation.

Anything is a good enough subject for drawing-room comedy. But this comedy is untidy in construction, cluttered with clichés and nonentities and deficient in wit. . . . As they are volatile and skillful performers, "I Know My Love" recovers remarkably when they return. Mr. Lunt struts and Miss Fontaine looks slyly wise—a situation that is gay and shining in the incomparable Lunt tradition. They have a fond, quizzical scene at the close in their most immaculate style. But to one astonished theatergoer, the gleams of witty acting after the first act do not sufficiently compensate for an increasingly muddled play. . . .

All this would have sailed over the impatient Holden's head, caught between "horsing around" with Sally in cabs and hating the phoniness she and the Lunts are meant to embody. Holden could no more resist the movies than he could allow himself to genuinely enjoy them. Such is the stuff of which his ongoing neurosis—and unstinting cultural critique—is made. The movies pile up images calculated to tap our emotions and to move them in orchestrated, predictable ways; and the silly Broadway vehicles in which the Lunts often starred bear little (or no) relationship to life. About the former, Holden falls into a mimickry that suggests how deeply formative the images found in movies are (for example, Humphrey Bogart continually hitching up his pants in *High Sierra* or James Cagney shouting ''Top of the world, Ma'' in the concluding scene of *White Heat*). As for the latter, Holden pretty much suffers his way through Broadway performances knowing that phonies admire them, and he does not. In short, Holden will have none of this pretentiousness, preferring instead the honesty of his own impressions. Is he being unfair? Absolutely. Is he onto something? Again, absolutely. Indeed, this important subtheme in *The Catcher in the Rye* speaks volumes about issues that are ongoing in a culture that wonders how much on-screen violence and loosened morals our nation—and especially its youth—can stand. If Holden is notable for trying (unsuccessfully) to erase the verbal filth from schoolroom walls, one can only imagine what he would think (and do?) about many current Hollywood blockbusters.

STUDY QUESTIONS

1. Holden is quoted as saying, "If there's one thing I hate, it's the movies. Don't even mention them to me." In fact, Holden not only mentions movies himself but also patterns his behavior on some of them. As stated in this chapter, he imagines himself in a scene from a gangster film and musical. If *The Catcher in the Rye* were rewritten to fit into our current time frame, what films might Holden use to replace the ones mentioned in the chapter?

2. As with many other things, Holden thinks the movies are "phony." Compile a list of Holden's arguments to support his claims against the movies.

3. Using the list you have just compiled, analyze Holden's behavior to see if it supported his arguments, or if he acted hypocritically.

4. Based on Holden's opinion of film, what would he think about television?

5. Imagine you are writing the screenplay of *The Catcher in the Rye*. Compile a list of any changes you think would be necessary to translate the novel to the medium of film. If you think the novel can be transformed into a movie without any changes, explain why.

6. Obtain a tape of one of the films mentioned in *The Catcher in the Rye*. Analyze the film in terms of being phony for yourself.

TOPICS FOR WRITTEN OR ORAL EXPLORATION

1. Hemingway and Salinger had similar opinions about film. However, many of Hemingway's novels were made into movies. Read a Hemingway novel that was made into a film and compare it with the film. Write a paper on whether or not the film corrupted the author's written version of the story.

2. Research the popular films for the last five years. Write a paper to support or refute Holden's claims that movies are "phony," using modern films to prove your point of view.

SUGGESTED READINGS

Brown, Jared. *The Fabulous Lunts*. New York: Atheneum, 1986. A biography of Alfred Lunt and Lynn Fontanne that also provides a close look at Broadway theater during the years covered in *The Catcher in the Rye*.

Clarens, Carlos. *Crime Movies: An Illustrated History*. New York: W. W. Norton, 1980. Probably the most interesting and accessible book to deal with the impact of the gangster figure on Hollywood movies.

Gordon, Lois, and Alan Gordon, eds. *American Chronicle: Six Decades in American Life, 1920–1980*. New York: Atheneum, 1987. This highly useful reference work contains a year-by-year account of historical events, scientific discoveries, economic data, slang expressions, advertising slogans, technological breakthroughs, sports, theater, classical and popular music, film, and much more.

6 —————————————————————————————

Holden Caulfield on the Analyst's Couch

Holden relates his "madman weekend" in Manhattan from the vantage point of a rest home in California. He is exhausted both physically and mentally. Indeed, "breakdown" is the all-purpose term often used to describe somebody in Holden's shaky condition. Earlier in the novel Mr. Antolini, in an effort to give Holden some reality instruction in maturity, quotes from William Stekel, a disciple of Sigmund Freud: "The mark of the immature man is that he wants to die nobly for a cause, while the mark of the mature man is that he wants to live humbly for one." In a very few words Stekel puts his finger on the essential difference between romantic posturing and tragic wisdom; but the highly agitated, very confused Holden is too impatient to understand the point that Mr. Antolini is trying to make.

Later, when Holden imagines that Mr. Antolini has made a homosexual pass, he makes an abrupt exit only to find himself wondering if his snap judgment about a formerly revered teacher might be wrong. Rather than the simplistic division that pits those who are phony against those who are pure, Holden now finds himself smack up against a complicated, morally complex situation. After all, Mr. Antolini had covered the battered corpse of James Castle with his sports coat (reminding us of Holden's earlier worry that he might also jump to his own death), even though Mr. Antolini did not "catch" James Castle as Holden imagines he will do when standing at the edge of the cliff, and little children get too close to the edge. He, as the novel suggests, will be the *catcher* in the rye.

Still, Mr. Antolini—by Holden's own admission—was the best teacher he ever had, and, seeing Holden in such a sorry state, he delivers a stump speech (meant to contrast with those of the passive-aggressive Mr. Spencer) that is filled with ominous suggestions about Holden's heading toward a very special fall, one reserved for people who once looked for something that the world could not supply and who finally gave up looking altogether. Here, Mr. Antolini makes sound sense in his simultaneously gentle and no-nonsense way. But even he missed the psychoanalytic point, that Holden is nearly at the end of his physical tether and needs a warm bed far more than he does a good talking to. Furthermore, the whole issue of getting back on the straight-and-narrow academic track (the object of his well-meaning sermonizing) should wait until Holden loosens his grip on his pristine dreams and begins the difficult, complex task of engineering a separate peace with the larger world.

What Holden initially sees as a homosexual pass only complicates the situation, for Salinger renders the scene in ways that provide as much ammunition for those who regard Antolini as a pervert as it does for those who regard Holden as mistaken. After all, when his old teacher pats Holden's hair, couldn't this act be reckoned as one of sympathy, of caring and not in the least sordid? Holden doesn't think so at the time, and it is his startled accusations—or near accusations—that so rattle Mr. Antolini. There is little question that, in this scene, Holden is cast in the role of accuser. But since his narrative is studded with references to those he writes off as "flits," one has good reason to be skeptical about his hair-trigger judgments. Not that Holden is a homophobe, as the term is currently defined, or even that he speaks about homosexuality with the same deep conviction with which he ladles out pronouncements about writers, Ivy Leaguers, or adults in general. Indeed, Holden would be the first to admit that he is deeply confused about who is or is not a homosexual—much less about how one ought to properly process that information.

In this regard, one of his memories of life at Whooten School deserves special mention. Carl Luce, his student adviser, used to hold court on the one topic certain to gather an eager prep school crowd: sex. As Holden remembers it, Luce took perversion as his general province and made homosexuality his speciality. He knew every gay and lesbian hiding out in his and her respective closet, and Luce took a particular thrill in exposing a wide range of actors, actresses, and assorted public figures. Holden adds this to his storehouse of knowledge and, not surprisingly, to his mounting list of worries. If it were true, as Luce insisted, that a person could turn homosexual overnight, could that happen to *him*? Even scarier, what would he do about it if such a thing happened? Later, Mr. Antolini puts these unresolved inner conflicts into bold relief; and as dark concerns keep mounting up—his realization, for example, that he must allow Phoebe to reach for the brass ring even if she "falls" in the process—the world no longer seems as simple as it did when he announced his life's mission as a catcher in the rye.

Nor do things improve at the West Coast rest home, where (as Holden characteristically puts it) "[a] lot of people, especially this one psychoanalyst guy they have here, keeps asking me if I'm going to apply myself when I go back to school next September" (192). But, as Holden insists, how can people know, *really* know, what they're going to do until they *do* it? He might apply himself like crazy when he shows up at yet another prep school. The rub is that he can't be sure—and neither can anyone else.

In creating a multifaceted character such as Holden, Salinger is uninterested in psychological theories. For him, Holden was decidedly *not* crazy (whatever the term may mean to various members of the psychology community); and when a publisher so characterized Holden, he promptly pulled the manuscript out of editorial consideration.

Nonetheless, a wide range of psychological ideas can be applied to Holden's "case," although certain cautions are worth pointing out. In much the same way that Holden wrongly imagines that he might have cancer after reading a magazine article about "how you can tell if you have cancer or not," one can imagine him as a candidate for every condition explored in psychology textbooks. He is, for example, a world-class worrier and a first-rate neurotic. He alternates between feelings of superiority and inferiority; he fancies himself as quite a lady's man only to realize, at moments, how lonely he is. He wants to save the world at the same time he wants to escape from it. He is as passive as he is aggressive, as self-righteous as he is compassionate. In short, Holden is a study in adolescent confusion; and because he is a character in a novel (as opposed to an actual person), efforts to put him on the analyst's couch, determine the label that best fits his condition ("manic-depressive"? "martyr complex"? "regressive temperament"?), and then *cure* him are rather beside the point. There is evidence in the novel for nearly any psychological theory one might wish to impose on Holden.

Given all this, the best approach is to raise some general issues that confront readers of Salinger's novel and then follow these queries with a variety of opinions by experts in child psychology. Arguably, the most important question one can ask about oneself is, Who am I? Another, first posed by Socrates, is, How should a good person live? The two queries are more related than they might appear to be at first glance. Imagine the difficulties that Holden would have with the first question. He would surely not define himself as a Pencey student, not only for the very good reason that he has been kicked out but also because Holden rejects the definitions of "preppy" that Pencey—and other preparatory schools—want to impose. He would also have difficulties seeing himself as his father's son, especially since he is in rebellion against everything that signifies material success. The list could go on and on—yet another measure of *The Catcher in the Rye*'s greatness.

Even though Holden tries (unsuccessfully) to ape adult behavior, he realizes full well that he is an adolescent—still living in his parent's home (despite his romantic dreams of taking off for an ill-defined West), depending on the parental hands that feed him (and that he then metaphorically bites), and so relieved of any responsibilities that he has an endless amount of leisure time to dwell on how lonely he is and on how crappy the world has become.

HOLDEN THE ADOLESCENT

Holden is a textbook study in adolescent angst. To be more precise about how psychologists define "adolescence" (today's society defines it generally as the years between twelve and eighteen), the following documents discuss how a number of psychologists view adolescence and the importance of that stage on the development of the self.

FROM CARL R. GREEN AND WILLIAM R. SANFORD, "WHAT IS ADOLESCENCE?" IN *PSYCHOLOGY: A WAY TO GROW* (Amsco School Publications, Inc., 1982)

Psychologists agree that adolescence is a state of mind as well as a physical reality. For some young people, it's a time of rapid and exciting growth. After all, the term "adolescence" comes from the Latin verb *adolescere*, "to grow up." That's how sixteen-year-old Maria K. sees it:

> I can hardly wait to start each day. There's always something exciting to do, something new to learn. My parents give me a lot more freedom, and my boyfriend and I get along great. Also, since I decided to be a paramedic, school makes a lot more sense. Sure, it bugs me that some adults still treat me like a little kid. But I'm not in any rush to grow up. I'm having a good time right now.

Other adolescents find it difficult to make sense out of their new physical maturity. Suddenly, the world seems to close in on them. As Hammond A. says,

> I wasn't prepared for all the crazy feelings that go through my mind. Sometimes I feel OK, but other times I feel like dying. Girls scare me, and I can't seem to talk to my folks anymore. It's like having a bomb inside me that might go off any minute. I wish people would get off my back and just leave me alone.

Hammond A. would surely read *The Catcher in the Rye* with a good deal of empathy because Holden, too, is riddled with "crazy feelings" and a profound wish to be left alone. As for Maria K., we suspect that she would join those who are perplexed by Holden's profound unhappiness and deeply rebellious behavior. She might even point out that Holden's life, all things considered, doesn't look so bad to her and that if he would just quit whining, he could make something of himself.

As Green and Sanford put it: "Why do some people seem to coast through adolescence, while others find it a constant struggle to keep their heads above water?" *The Catcher in the Rye* posits some tentative answers about the latter group, albeit not with the methodological precision so essential to psychology. Rather, Salinger's novel is at once a dramatization of how a given fictional character thinks, acts, and, most of all, *speaks*. In this regard, Holden's voice is simultaneously individual and collective, for his war against phoniness in all its varied forms defines him at the same time that it (partially) identifies us.

FROM ANN L. WEBER, *INTRODUCTION TO PSYCHOLOGY*
(New York: HarperPerennial, 1991)

As a stage of development, adolescence is greatly influenced by one's culture. In more primitive societies, for example, the transition from childhood to adulthood is rapid and marked by traditionally prescribed rites of passage. . . . In American and European societies, the transition period has been steadily increasing over the past one hundred years, giving rise to a specific adolescent subculture. In addition, the conflicting signals regarding when one truly becomes an adult contribute to a variety of stress-related problems.

There are group and individual differences in the ages when these changes occur. For example, changes generally appear earlier in girls than boys, and earlier in southern as compared to northern climates.

At present the mechanism determining the actual timing of the changes is unknown. It is clear, however, that being an individual at either extreme of the age range for one's group is psychologically stressful.

Girls typically begin the height and weight growth spurt around age ten, reach a peak at about twelve, and decelerate markedly by fourteen. The spurt occurs almost two years later in boys; thus, girls are typically taller and heavier than boys from about ten and a half to thirteen.

The growth spurt also changes both body proportions and body shape, a source of embarrassment and concern for many adolescents. Arms and legs grow rapidly, sometimes producing a temporary awkwardness or clumsiness. Chest and shoulder tissue grows rapidly in boys, as does hip and thigh tissue in girls. Adolescents concerned about these changes in body build may diet or exercise compulsively in an effort to regain what they view as an attractive shape. Serious eating disorders such as *anorexia* (abnormal fasting and self-starvation) may emerge at this stage.

In girls, enlargement of the breasts is usually the first external sign of impending puberty. The age of onset of menstruation, along with the age of onset of other physical changes, has been steadily decreasing for the past hundred years. Most girls today reach menarche, the first menstrual cycle, within six months of their thirteenth birthday, as compared to between ages fifteen–seventeen a century ago.

Boys typically begin their growth spurts at about twelve and a half. Impending sexual maturation is marked by enlargement of the testes, scrotum, and penis and the development of pubic hair. This is followed by enlargement of the larynx and thickening of the vocal cords, producing a transitional period in which the voice may "crack."

Adolescence is characterized by increases in ability to generalize, handle abstract ideas, and reason logically and consistently. These changes may reflect the emergence of a specific cognitive stage or the result of accumulating knowledge that expands one's capacity for making distinctions and inferring relationships. . . .

Becoming an adult requires establishing new relationships with parents and peers, and developing a sense of personal identity.

Some psychologists conceptualize the tasks of adulthood as a process of separation-individuation, a process of distancing oneself from parents and establishing a sense of individuality. Much has been written over the years about the "generation gap" (the perceived divergence between adolescents' values and those of their parents) and the tendency of adolescents to be over-influenced by their peers.

Research indicates that, in fact, parents and peers influence different spheres of adolescent life. Adolescents do experience and give in to peer pressure to conform, especially around puberty; but peers tend to influence adolescent decisions about superficial matters like dress, language, and recreation. Parents usually continue to influence adolescent values and long-term goals. In fact, the basic values of most adolescents' friends are quite similar to those of their parents, possibly because adolescents' friendship choices are influenced by values learned at home.

With the onset of puberty, adolescents become sexual beings. The past twenty-five years have seen marked changes in adolescent sexual attitudes and behavior. Most adolescents now view premarital sex as acceptable if it occurs within the context of a loving relationship. By age nineteen, two-thirds of adolescent girls and four-fifths of adolescent boys have had sexual intercourse.

Sexuality can be viewed as part of establishing a more adult identity. Erikson saw adolescence as precipitating an identity crisis, a period when one reevaluates oneself with an eye toward entering the adult world. Adolescence brings dramatic physical and cognitive changes that can disrupt childhood self-image. Adolescents must come to terms with their adult-like bodies and with the impending tasks of adulthood. Cognitive changes enable the adolescent to consider the relationship between "who I am" and "who I want to be." Typically, establishing an identity involves adopting a sense of personal values and making an initial vocational decision. Adolescents who are unable to resolve these issues are viewed as experiencing diffusion as an incomplete sense of reality.

FROM JAMES MARCIA, "ADOLESCENCE," IN
PSYCHOLOGY & YOU
(Teacher's edition, 2nd ed., Frank B. McMahon, Judith W.
McMahon, and Tony Romano, eds. St. Paul, Minn.: West Publishing
Company, 1995)

. . . Erik Erikson emphasizes the importance of forming an individual identity in his theory of personality development. According to his theory, from approximately age 12 until at least the end of the teenage years, accurately defining the "self" is our major task. Belonging to a group is the first step. The next step is seeing how you are different from that group, how you are a unique person. Developing a sense of yourself as an individual means achieving *identity* [usually defined as a sense of oneself as a unique person]. Never reaching this goal results in *identity confusion* [Erikson's term for an uncertainty about who one is or where one is going; Holden seriously suffers from this condition].

For Erikson, adolescence represents a crossroads, a time of upheaval, of selecting from many possibilities the ones that fit. This is not easy to do. As a result, adolescence is not an easy time. Too many decisions are forced on the adolescent too quickly. He or she must not only define the self and learn how to relate to the other sex but also make plans about occupations to pursue. Because these decisions have long-range consequences, they create a lot of anxiety and insecurity.

It is natural for youth to flounder around, going back and forth before completing this task. Most adolescents experiment with a variety of roles, discarding one to try out another. In their search, some will identify with a public figure, perhaps an actor, actress, or rock star, taking his or her mannerisms and style of dress, at least for a while.

Delaying the usual commitments of adulthood to find one's identity is called a *moratorium* (meaning a period of "time out"). In our society, this means that adolescents can engage in behaviors that are not allowed for adults. An obvious example is that teenagers are not expected to marry, start a family, or support themselves. On the other hand, think of how your community would react to a group of adults who dressed like teenagers and drove around the local hamburger place hanging out the car windows, shouting and waving at people they know. Moratorium is definitely reserved for adolescents. (317–20)

Granted, Salinger did not write his portrait of Holden Caulfield with Erikson's theories of adolescent "identity" in mind, but it is interesting to note how much crossover there seems to be. As a novelist Salinger needs to dramatize these tensions rather than to talk about them in abstract language. To understand this important difference, one need only revisit the passage in *The Catcher in the Rye* where Holden describes himself as a seventeen-year-old who sometimes acts as if he were thirteen. Nor does his elaborate tapestry of contradictions end there: "It's really ironical," Holden points out, because "I'm six foot two and a half and I have gray hair. . . . And yet I still act sometimes like I was only about twelve. Sometimes I act a lot older than I am—I really do—but people never notice it. People never notice anything" (12). Holden's defensiveness is connected to his deep-seated anxieties about identity—in this case, about whether he is every inch the adult (he isn't, as his pathetic attempts to be served alcohol show), or whether he is much younger than his gray hairs suggest. Erikson's general notions about adolescents and identity were expanded by the research of James Marcia. He divided the identity crisis (and here Holden is a prime candidate for one) into four states.

FROM JAMES MARCIA, "ADOLESCENCE," IN
PSYCHOLOGY & YOU
(Teacher's edition, 2nd ed., Frank B. McMahon, Judith W.
McMahon, and Tony Romano, eds. St. Paul, Minn.: West Publishing
Company, 1995)

IDENTITY FORECLOSURE

Adolescents who simply accept the identity and values they were given in childhood are in a state of *foreclosure* (not giving themselves a chance to explore alternatives). They have not experimented with other possibilities before deciding who they are. Instead, their self-concept has been defined by other people. For some adolescents, a *negative identity* [Marcia's term for defining oneself as "bad" or a "troublemaker"] results from foreclosure. These are the kids who were labeled *bad* or *troublemakers* in childhood and who have come to accept the label. Whether the identity is negative or not, foreclosure means blocking off certain possibilities for growth and individuality.

IDENTITY DIFFUSION

Adolescents who don't have a clear idea of their identity *and* are not trying to find one are in a state of *diffusion* [Marcia's term for the state of having no clear idea of one's identity]. These adolescents may have struggled with the issue of identity in the past, but they never resolved it, and they seem to have stopped trying. The outcome is a lack of self-identity and no real commitment to values or personal goals.

MORATORIUM

Adolescents who are trying to achieve an identity through experimentation and trial and error are in a state of *moratorium.* . . . Adolescents remaining in moratorium or time out may or may not achieve a sense of identity. Some give up the struggle and wind up in a state of diffusion.

IDENTITY ACHIEVEMENT

Adolescents who have gone through the identity crisis and come out with a well-defined self-concept, who are committed to a set of personal values, beliefs, and goals, have reached the state of *identity achievement*. Their identities may be expanded and further defined in adulthood, but the basics are there, and such adolescents are well prepared to make meaningful lives for themselves. (320–22)

Literary critics sometimes talk about *The Catcher in the Rye* as an initiation novel and concentrate on those moments where Holden most seems to be on "a journey of learning." Certainly, his travels both to Manhattan and around its streets are suggestive of this, along with his fantasies of traveling westward to a place notable for its absence of phonies. However, in Marcia's terminology Holden seems to be a profile in diffusion, neither very clear about who he is nor much interested in making productive efforts to find out. Indeed, one suspects that Holden would regard Marcia's characterizations with the same skepticism that he brings to the psychoanalyst who keeps asking about what he plans to do in yet another new school next September: "It's a stupid question, in my opinion. I mean how do you know what you're going to do till you *do* it?" (213). Those evidencing a healthy "identity achievement" would answer the doctor's question quite differently.

ADOLESCENCE THEN AND NOW

One slangy way of describing Holden's erratic behavior might be to say that he is "stressed out." But situational stress is a slippery concept, not only because there are wide differences of opinion about precisely what *stress* is (what some cope with relatively easily, others find overwhelming) but also because what our culture considers as stress has changed significantly since the days when Holden discovered phoniness (and his attendant disgust) everywhere he looked. Like much else, innocence is not what it used to be. According to a 1989 survey of high school seniors in forty Wisconsin communities, a top-ten list of contemporary teenager worries would look like this:

1. Having a good marriage and family life.
2. Choosing a career/finding steady work.
3. Doing well in school.
4. Being successful in line of work.
5. Having strong friendships.
6. Paying for college.
7. The country's going downhill.
8. Making a lot of money.
9. Finding a purpose and meaning in life.
10. Contracting AIDS.

By contrast, Holden's top-ten list would probably be restricted to a single, overwhelming item: how to avoid becoming a phony. As his paraphrase of Hamlet's soliloquy would have it: To be or not to be a phony, *that* is the question. No doubt he would regard the worries that his contemporary counterparts ruminate about as the stuff of which future phonies are made: doing well in school, being successful at one's job, making a pile of money. For somebody who dreams about being a "catcher in the rye," a savior of young children who might "fall," Holden's agenda is as unrealistic as it is (in many ways) commendable. It does not square, however, with surveys polling real teenagers, either in Holden's day or our own.

To better appreciate the psychological distance between the world of adolescents as presented in Salinger's novel and that of the present, we provide the following extended excerpt. Its emphasis may be on problems (for example, divorce, drugs, sexually active behavior and consequences) that Holden Caulfield did not directly face, but thinking about what a Holden-type might say and do in the 1990s is worth consideration.

FROM DAVID GELMAN, "A MUCH RISKIER PASSAGE"
(*Newsweek*, summer/fall, 1990)

There was a time when teenagers believed themselves to be part of a conquering army. Through much of the 1960s and 1970s, the legions of adolescents appeared to command the center of American culture like a victorious occupying force, imposing their singular tastes in clothing, music, and recreational drugs on a good many of the rest of us. It was a hegemony buttressed by advertisers, fashion setters, record producers suddenly zeroing in on the teen multitudes as if they controlled the best part of the nation's wealth, which in some sense they did. But even more than market power, what made the young insurgents invincible was the conviction that they were right: from the crusade of the children, grown-ups believe, they must learn to trust their feelings, to shun materialism, to make love, not money.

In 1990 the emblems of rebellion that once set teenagers apart have grown frayed. Their music now seems more derivative than subversive. The provocative teenage styles of dress that adults assiduously copied no longer automatically inspire emulation. And underneath the plumage, teens seem to be more interested in getting ahead in the world than in clearing up its injustices. . . .

One reason today's teens aren't shaking the earth is that they can no longer marshal the demographic might they once could. Although their sheer numbers are still growing, they are not the illimitable expanding force that teens appeared to be twenty years ago. In 1990 they constituted a smaller percentage of the total population (7 percent, compared with nearly 10 percent in 1970). For another thing, almost as suddenly as they become a highly visible, if unlikely, power in the world, teenagers have reverted to anonymity and the old search for identity. Author Todd Gitlin, a chronicler of the '60s, believes that they have become "Balkanized," united less by a common culture than by the commodities they own. He says "it's impossible to point to an overarching teen sensibility."

But as a generation, today's teenagers face more adult-strength stresses than their predecessors did—at a time when adults are much less available to help them. With the divorce rate hovering near fifty percent, and forty to fifty percent of teenagers living in single-parent homes headed mainly by working mothers, teens are more on their own than ever. "My parents let me do anything I want as long as I don't get into trouble," writes a fifteen-year-old high-schooler from Ohio in an essay submitted for this special issue of *Newsweek*. Sociologists have begun to realize, in fact, that teens are more dependent on grown-ups than was once believed. Studies indicate that they are shaped more by their parents than their peers, that they adopt their parents' values and opinions to a greater extent than anyone realized. Adolescent specialists now see real hazards in lumping all teens together; thirteen-year-olds, for instance, need much more parental guidance than nineteen-year-olds.

These realizations are emerging just when the world has become a more dangerous place for the young. They have more access than ever to fast cars, fast drugs, easy sex—"a bewildering array of options, many with devastating outcomes," observes Beatrix Hamburg, director of Child and Adolescent Psychiatry at New York's Mt. Sinai School of Medicine. Studies indicate that while overall drug abuse is down, the use of lethal drugs like crack is up in low-income neighborhoods, and a dangerous new kick called ice is making inroads in white high schools. Drinking and smoking rates remain ominously high. "The use of alcohol appears to be normative," says Stephen Small, a developmental psychologist at the University of Wisconsin, "By the upper grades, everybody's doing it."

Sexual activity is also on the rise. A poll conducted by Small suggests that most teens are regularly having sexual intercourse by the eleventh grade. Parents are generally surprised by the data. Small says, "A lot of parents are saying, 'Not my kids. . . . ' They just don't think it's happening." Yet clearly it is: around half a million teenage girls give birth every year, and sexually transmitted diseases continue to be a major problem. Perhaps the only comforting note is that teens who are given AIDS education in schools and clinics are more apt to use condoms—a practice that could scarcely be mentioned a few years ago, let alone surveyed.

One reliable assessment of how stressful life has become for young people in this country is the Index of Social Health for Children and Youth. Authored by social-policy analyst Marc Miringoff, of Fordham University at Tarrytown, N.Y., it charts such factors as poverty, drug-abuse, and high-school dropout rates. In 1987, the latest year for which statistics are available, the index fell to its lowest point in two decades. Most devastating, according to Miringoff, were the numbers of teenagers living at poverty levels—about fifty-five percent for single-parent households—and taking their own lives. The record rate of nearly eighteen suicides per 100,000 in 1987—a total of 1,901—was double that of 1970. "If you take teens in the '50s—the 'Ozzie and Harriet' generation [as well as that of Holden Caulfield]—those kids lived on a less complex planet," says Miringoff. "They could be kids longer."

The social index is only one of the yardsticks used on kids today. In fact, this generation of young people is surely one of the most closely watched ever. Social scientists are tracking nearly everything they do or think about, from dating habits (they prefer going out in groups) to extracurricular activities (cheerleading has made a comeback) to general outlook (45 percent think the world is getting worse and 62 percent believe life will be harder for them than it was for their parents). One diligent prober, Reed Larson of the University of Illinois, even equipped his 500 teen subjects with beepers so he could remind them to fill out questionnaires about how they are feeling, what they are doing and who they are with at random moments during the day. Larson, a professor of human development, and Maryse Richards of Loyola University have followed this group since grade school. Although the results of the high-school study have not been tabulated yet, the assumption is that young people are experiencing more stress by the time they reach adolescence but develop strategies to cope with it.

Without doubt, any overview of teenage problems is skewed by the experiences of the inner cities, where most indicators tilt sharply toward the negative. Especially among the minority poor, teen pregnancies continue to rise, while the institution of marriage has virtually disappeared. According to the National Center for Vital Statistics, 90 percent of black teenage mothers are unmarried at the time of their child's birth, although about a third eventually marry. Teenage mothers, in turn, add to the annual school-dropout rate, which in some cities reaches as high as 60 percent. Nationwide, the unemployment rate for black teenagers is 40 to 50 percent; in some cities, it has risen to seventy percent. Crack has become a medium of commerce and violence. "The impact of crack is worse in the inner city than anywhere else," says psychiatrist Robert King of the Yale Child Study Center. "If you look at the homicide rate among young black males, it's frighteningly high. We also see large numbers of young mothers taking crack."

Those are realities unknown to the majority of white middle-class teenagers. Most of them are managing to get through the adolescent years with relatively few major problems. Parents may describe them as sullen and self-absorbed [Holden could be described in much the same way]. They can also be secretive and rude. They hang "Do Not Disturb" signs on their doors, make phone calls from closets and behave churlishly at the dinner table if they can bring themselves to sit there at all. An earlier beeper study by Illinois's Larson found that in the period between ages ten and fifteen, the amount of time young people spend with their families decreases by half. "This is when the bedroom door becomes a significant marker," he says.

Yet their rebelliousness is usually overstated. "Arguments are generally about whether to take out the garbage or whether to wear a certain hairstyle," says Bradford Brown, an associate professor of human development at the University of Wisconsin. "These are not earth-shattering issues, though they are quite irritating to parents." One researcher on a mission to destigmatize teenagers is Northeastern University professor Ken Howard, author of a book, "The Teenage World," who has just completed a study in Chicago's Cook County on where kids go for help. The perception, says Howard, is that teenagers are far worse off than they really are. He believes that their emotional disturbances are no different from those of adults, and that it is only 20 percent who have most of the serious problems, in any case.

The findings of broad-based studies of teenagers often obscure the differences in these experiences. They are, after all, the product of varied ethical and cultural influences. Observing adolescents in ten communities over the last ten years, a team of researchers headed by Frances Ianni, of Columbia University's Teachers College, encountered "considerable diversity." A key finding, reported Ianni in a 1989 article in Phi Delta Kappan magazine, was that the people in all the localities reflected the ethnic and social-class lifestyles of their parents much more than that of a universal teen culture. The researchers found "far more congruence than conflict" between the views of parents and their teenage children. "We much more frequently hear teenagers preface comments to their peers with 'my mom says' than with any attributions to heroes of the youth culture," wrote Ianni.

For years, psychologists also tended to overlook the differences between younger and older adolescents, instead grouping them together as if they all had the same needs and desires. Until a decade ago, ideas of teen behavior were heavily influenced by the work of psychologist Erik Erikson, whose own model was based on older adolescents. Erikson, for example, emphasized their need for autonomy—appropriate, perhaps, for an eighteen-year-old preparing to leave home for college or a job, but hardly for a thirteen-year-old just beginning to experience the confusions of puberty. The Erikson model nevertheless was taken as an across-the-board prescription to give teenagers independence, something that families, torn by the domestic upheavals of the '80s and '70s, granted them almost by forfeit.

That period helped plant the belief that adolescents were natural rebels who sought above all to break free of adult influences. The idea persists to this day. Says Ruby Takanishi, director of the Carnegie Council of Adolescent Development: "The society is still permeated by the notion that adolescents are different, that their hormones are raging around and they don't want anything to do with their parents or other adults." Yet research by Ianni and others suggests the contrary. Ianni points also to studies of so-called invulnerable adolescents—those who develop into stable young adults in spite of coming from troubled homes, or other adversity. "A lot of people have attributed this to some inner resilience," he says. "But what we've seen in practically all cases is some caring adult figure who was a constant in that kid's life."

Not that teenagers were always so dependent on adults. Until the mid-nineteenth century, children labored in the fields alongside their parents. But by the time they were fifteen, they might marry and go out into the world. Industrialization and compulsory education ultimately deprived them of a role in the family work unit, leaving them in a state of suspension between childhood and adulthood.

To teenagers, it has always seemed a useless period of waiting. Approaching physical and sexual maturity, they feel capable of doing many of the things adults do. But they are not treated like adults. Instead they must endure a prolonged childhood that is stretched out even more nowadays by the need to attend college—and then possibly graduate school—in order to make one's way in the world. In the family table of organization, they are mainly in charge of menial chores. Millions of teenagers now have part-time or full-time jobs, but those tend to be in the service industries, where the pay and the work are only equally unrewarding.

If teenagers are to stop feeling irrelevant, they need to feel needed, both by the family and by the larger world. In the '60s they gained some sense of empowerment from their visibility, their music, their sheer collective noise. They also joined and swelled the ranks of Vietnam War protesters, giving them a feeling of importance that evidently they have not had since. In the foreword to "Student Services," a book based on a 1985 Carnegie Foundation survey of teenagers' attitudes toward work and community service, foundation director Ernest Boyer wrote: "Time and time again, students complained that they felt isolated, unconnected to the larger world. . . . And this detachment occurs at the very time students are deciding who they are and where they fit." Fordham's Miringoff goes so far as to link the rising suicide rate among teens to their feelings of disconnection. He recalls going to the 1963 March on Washington as a teenager and gaining "a sense of being part of something larger. That idealism, that energy, was a very stabilizing thing."

Surely there is still room for idealism in the '90s, even if the causes are considered less glamorous. But despite growing instances of teenagers involving themselves in good works, such as recycling campaigns, tutorial programs or serving meals at shelters for the homeless, no study has detected anything like a national ground swell of volunteerism. Instead, according to University of Michigan social psychologist Lloyd Johnston, teens seem to be taking their cue from a culture that, up until quite recently at least, has glorified self-interest and opportunism. "It's fair to say that young people are more career oriented than before, more concerned about making money and prestige," says Johnson. "These changes are consistent with the Me Generation and looking for the good life they see on television."

Some researchers say that, indeed, the only thing uniting teenagers these days are the things they buy and plug into. Rich or poor, all have their Walkmans, their own VCRs and TVs. Yet in some ways, those marvels of communication isolate them even more. Teenagers, says Beatrix Hamburg, are spending "a lot of time alone in their rooms." [Computer games and surfing the Internet have only complicated this phenomenon in recent years. For better or worse, Holden was spared these temptations—although one could argue that he was as "isolated" as are his contemporary counterparts.]

Other forces may be working to isolate them as well. According to Dr. Elena O. Nightingale, author of a Carnegie Council paper on teen rolelessness, a pattern of "age segregation" is shrinking the amount of time adolescents spend with grown-ups. In place of family outings and vacations, for example, entertainment is now more geared toward age-specific groups. (The teen-terrorizing "Freddy" flicks and their ilk would be one example.) Even in the sorts of jobs typically available to teenagers, such as fast-food chains, they are usually supervised by people close to their age, rather than by adults, notes Nightingale. "There's a real need for places for teenagers to go where there's a modicum of adult involvement," she says.

Despite the riskier world they face, it would be a mistake to suggest that all adolescents of this generation are feeling more angst than their predecessors. Middle-class teenagers, at least, seem content with their lot on the whole: According to recent studies, 80 percent—the same proportion as twenty years ago—profess satisfaction with their own lives, if not with the state of the world. Many teenagers, nonetheless, evince wistfulness for what they think of as a more heroic times in the '60s and '70s—an era, they believe, when teenagers had more say in the world. Playwright Wendy Wasserstein, whose Pulitzer Prize-winning "The Heidi Chronicles" was about coming of age in those years, says she has noticed at least a "stylistic" nostalgia in the appearance of peace-sign earrings and other '60s artifacts. "I guess that comes from the sense of there having been a unity, a togetherness," she says. "Today most teens are wondering about what they're going to do when they grow up. We had more of a sense of liberation, of youth—we weren't thinking about getting that job at Drexel." Pop-culture critic Greil Marcus, however, believes it was merely the "self-importance" of the '60s generation—his own contemporaries—"that has oppressed today's kids into believing they've missed something. There's something sick about my eighteen-year-old daughter wanting to see Paul McCartney or the Who. We would never have emulated our parents' culture."

But perhaps that's the point: the teens of the '90s do emulate the culture of their parents, many of whom are the very teens who once made such an impact on their own parents. These parents no doubt have something very useful to pass on to their children—and maybe their lost sense of idealism rather than the preoccupation with going and getting that seems, so far, their main legacy to the young. Mom and Dad have to earn a living and fulfill their own needs—they are not likely to be coming home early. But there must be a time and place for them to give their children the advice, the comfort, and, most of all, the feelings of possibility that any new generation needs in order to believe in itself.

Interestingly enough, Holden would probably not regard himself as a member of *any* peer grouping, just as many young adults later resented being called baby boomers, members of the "Me Generation," or, now, "Gen. Xers." Think, for example, of the moments in Salinger's novel when Holden rails against the shallow snobbishness of prep school cliques. In much the same way that he takes a certain amount of pleasure in *not* attending the big football game between Pencey and Saxon, Holden is skeptical about the ways that people of the same religion, income level, or social skill socialize together. At the same time Holden protests about all this just a bit too much; indeed, one could argue that he is lonely enough to have welcomed virtually any overture from virtually any Pencey clique. So far as we know, no psychologist has directly commented on this aspect of Holden's psychic makeup, but as Helen L. Bee and Sandra K. Mitchell suggest, peer interactions (both positive and negative) are an important part of adolescence.

FROM HELEN L. BEE AND SANDRA K. MITCHELL, *THE DEVELOPING PERSON: A LIFE-SPAN APPROACH*
(New York: HarperCollins, 1980)

Peer interactions among adolescents have many of the same qualities as those among younger children. The trend toward "gang" formation becomes very strong, and the gangs become more tightly knit and more significant for the individual teenager. These groups are mostly formed on the basis of shared backgrounds or interests, such as the "jocks," or the "bookworms." Teen groups also tend to be segregated along social class and racial lines. Furthermore . . . teen groups have strong norms and may have elaborate rituals, such as informal dress codes. [Here one might think of Holden's red hunting cap, self-consciously worn backward.]

Over the period from about age twelve to the end of high school, however, there is a major transition in the make-up of groups from same-sex to mixed-sex—to heterosexual pairs. . . . The "crowd" is a loosely organized group made up of young people who share the same activities or interests, including both boys and girls. Within the crowd there are smaller groups sometimes called "cliques," made up of young people with stronger ties to one another. At the beginning of adolescence, these cliques tend to be same-sex groups, but by later adolescence they may be made up of three or four couples who share many activities. Finally, the cliques may be made up of individual pairs of close friends or of "steady" couples.

These groups are extremely significant in the life of teenagers, particularly in the early years of adolescence when conformity to group norm is at its height. During high school, however, the dominance of the group declines somewhat. . . . We would expect that the child or young adolescent, whose moral reasoning is at the "conventional" level, would be more influenced by peer group norms and expectations than would the teenager who has moved to Stage 5 (the "autonomous level") of moral reasoning, and that is roughly what the data show.

Again, Holden would disagree with much of this psychologizing, and he would draw upon his experiences with conformist phonies for his examples. Indeed, *The Catcher in the Rye* is shot through with evidence of Holden's deep-seated quarrel with the world around him. To talk about most teenagers as capable of independent thinking just doesn't suggest that such people know what they're talking about.

On the other hand, psychologists would be especially attentive to Holden's interior monologue about suicide—yet another place where he and Hamlet cross paths:

I stayed in the bathroom [this after Maurice, the pimp, has punched him in the stomach] for about an hour, taking a bath and all. Then I got back in bed. It took me quite a while to get to sleep—I wasn't even tired—but finally I did. What I really felt like, though, was committing suicide. I felt like jumping out the window. I probably would've done it, too, if I'd been sure somebody'd cover me up as soon as I landed. I didn't want a bunch of stupid rubbernecks looking at me when I was all gory. (96)

That Holden soon finds himself at the end of his delicate psychological tether is true enough, but we can only speculate about his possible behavior beyond the information Salinger dramatizes in his pages. The psychologists we have cited might talk about Holden's successful progression through all the requisite stages of adolescent development sometime in the future. Perhaps, but as Mr. Antolini suggests, Holden also just might end up as the sort of person who sits in a bar hating people who look as if they might have played football in college or who mangle the grammatical niceties. Readers will no doubt differ about the life Holden might lead beyond the pages of Salinger's book (and there is nothing particularly wrong with these speculations, especially if proponents of one view or another offer up evidence from the text), but what Salinger has given us is a portrait of adolescence that remains, like the figures in the Natural Museum of History, frozen, unchanging, and yet coming to life once again whenever we turn the pages and hear, yet again, Holden's deeply affecting voice.

STUDY QUESTIONS

1. Mr. Antolini quotes William Stekel to Holden: "The mark of the immature man is that he wants to die nobly for a cause, while the mark of the mature man is that he wants to live humbly for one." What is he trying to get Holden to understand?

2. Is Holden a mature or immature man according to the quote? Explain your opinion, using examples from the novel.

3. Salinger doesn't "cure" Holden in his novel. Give your opinion why he ends the novel with Holden in the rest home.

4. The term "adolescence" comes from the Latin verb *adolescere*, "to grow up." Discuss the ways you think Holden shows signs of "growing up" during the novel. If you don't think he does any "growing up," explain if you think he should still be classified as an adolescent.

5. Holden is not one of the teenagers who seem to be coasting through adolescence. He seems to be having a constant struggle to keep his head above water. Cite the novel to support your opinion as to why Holden is having such a hard time.

6. Research indicates that peers' influence has great impact on adolescent life. Trace any peer influence you see impacting Holden's life. What, if any, parental influence can you trace?

7. Compare the attitudes toward adolescent sexual behavior of today's teenagers to those of Holden's generation by citing examples from the novel.

8. Erik Erikson theorized that adolescence precipitates identity crisis. An adolescent who doesn't develop a sense of self as an individual has *identity confusion*. Analyze Holden in terms of this theory by citing examples of his behavior from the novel.

9. James Marcia expanded on Erikson's theories by dividing the identity crisis into stages. Study the stages from this chapter and fit Holden into one or more of them. Justify your answer with examples from the text.

10. The chapter cites research that emphasizes adult influence as a key element in the healthy psychological and emotional development of adolescents. Comment on this research using examples from the novel to support your position. Discuss the statement in terms of the current time period.

TOPICS FOR WRITTEN OR ORAL EXPLORATION

1. Holden ponders the question put to him by the analyst when he is in the rest home, Will he apply himself when he is back in school the

next September? Holden isn't sure what he will do. Create that scenario by writing what will happen to Holden when he returns to
school.

2. Look up the word "neurotic" in terms of its psychological meaning.
Citing examples from the novel, determine if Holden fits the definition.

3. Adolescence is discussed in the chapter from a psychological perspective. One focus is how gender impacts on this period of development.
Review the chapter, research other psychological studies on adolescence, and discuss Holden's problems in terms of his gender. How
much of what Holden goes through is because he is a male? How
would the novel change if Holden were a girl?

4. Erik Erikson thought accurately defining the "self" is the teenager's
major task. Write a research paper that compares the difficulty of this
task for the teenagers of Holden's generation and the teenagers of
your generation.

SUGGESTED READINGS

Blos, Peter. *The Adolescent Personality: A Study of Individual Behavior
for the Commission on Secondary School Curriculum*. New York:
D. Appleton-Century, 1941.

Erikson, Erik. *Childhood and Society*. New York: Norton, 1964.

Horney, Karen. *Neuroses and Human Growth: The Struggle Toward Self-
Realization*. London: Routledge & Kegan Paul, 1951.

Maslow, Abraham. *Toward a Psychology of Being*. 3rd ed. New York: J.
Wiley & Sons, 1999.

Piaget, Jean. *The Development of Thought: Equilibrium of Cognitive
Structures*. New York: Viking Press, 1977.

Index

Gasdsen, Nate, 108–11
Gelman, David, 156–62
Georgia, 42–44
Glynn Academy (Georgia), 42–45
Go Ask Alice (anonymous), 44
Goldman, Rev. Curtis, 38
Golf, 5–6
Goodman, Paul, 77
Gordon, Kimberly, 42–44
Great Gatsby, The (Fitzgerald), 1
Great Ziegfeld, The (film), 131–32
Greenwich Village, 80, 89
Growing Up Absurd (Goodman), 77
Guare, John, 137

Habeus corpus, writ of, 56
Hamilton, Ian, 102
Hamlet (Shakespeare) (film), 130, 138–40
Hart, Jeffrey, 77
Hawthorne, Nathaniel, xvi
Hayes, Sally, 84, 86–87, 140
Hemingway, Ernest, 5, 129–30
Henry, Frederic, 5
High Sierra (film), 136
Hill, Fanny, 55, 62
Hobeck, John, 38
Holmes, Justice Oliver Wendell, 53
Holmes, Peter, 55, 65
Homosexuality, 19, 145–47
House Un-American Activities Committee (HUAC), 58, 78
Howard, Ken, 159
Hughes, Howard, 135–36
Hughes, Riley, 30
Hykes, Mrs. Alice, 37

Identity: achievement, 154; diffusion, 154; foreclosure, 153–54
I Know My Love (Behrman), 140–41

I Know Why the Caged Bird Sings (Angelou), 44, 49
Index for Social Health for Children and Youth (Miringoff), 157–58
Indiana, 41
In Our Time (Hemingway), 130
In Search of J. D. Salinger (Hamilton), 102
Introduction to Psychology (Weber), 150–52
Invisible Man, The (Ellison), 1
Irony, 48, 89, 153

Jazz, 80, 89–91
Jazz: A History of the New York Scene (Chartres and Kunstadt), 89–91
Jefferson, Thomas, 51, 56
Jenkinson, Edward B., 35
Jim (Huck Finn's friend), 3
Jones, Ernst, 139

Kansas, 38–41
Kaplan, Wes, 104–7
Kentucky, 35
Kerouac, Jack, 77–78
Knowles, John, 120–21
Kunstadt, Leonard, 89–91

Language: controversial, xvi; death imagery in, 2, 17; hyperbole, 2–3, 8; lies and exaggeration, 8–9; number of obscenities, 41, 46; slang, 8; teenage vernacular, 54
Lanier, Gene, 32
Lawrenceville School (New Jersey), 111–13
Leto, Justin, 42
Levin, Mrs. Beatrice, 35
Libel, 52–53, 67
Lincoln, Abraham, 56
Little Caesar (Zanuck) (film), 134

About the Authors

SANFORD PINSKER is Shadek Professor of Humanities at Franklin and Marshall College in Lancaster, Pennsylvania. He is the author of many books on American literature and culture.

ANN PINSKER teaches in the Social Studies Department of J. P. McCaskey High School in Lancaster, Pennsylvania. She is coordinator of McCaskey's International Baccalaureate Program.